TOUR DE FRANCE 100

A PHOTOGRAPHIC HISTORY OF CYCLING'S MOST ICONIC RACE

TOUR DE FRANCE 100

A PHOTOGRAPHIC HISTORY OF CYCLING'S MOST ICONIC RACE RICHARD MOORE

BLOOMSBURY

LONDON · NEW DELHI · NEW YORK · SYDNEY

Published 2013 by Bloomsbury Publishing Plc,
50 Bedford Square, London WC1B 3DP

ISBN (print) 978-1408-17096-0
ISBN (ePub) 978-1408-18683-1
ISBN (ePDF) 978-1408-18684-8

A CIP catalogue record for this book is available from
the British Library

This book is produced using paper that is made
from wood grown in managed sustainable forests.
It is natural, renewable and recyclable. The logging
and manufacturing processes conform to the
environmental regulations of the country of origin.

Design: XAB Design

Printed in China by C&C Offset Printing Co. Ltd.

10 9 8 7 6 5 4 3 2 1

Visit **www.bloomsbury.com** to find out more about
our authors and their books. You will find extracts,
author interviews and our blog, and you can sign up
for newsletters to be the first to hear about our latest
releases and special offers.

Contents

The front page of *L'Auto* on the morning of the first ever Tour de France, with the Tour's itinerary forming a rectangle in the hexagon shape of France. The Tour's founding newspaper was printed on yellow paper, which explained the colour of the race leader's jersey … though it was 16 years before the *maillot jaune* was adopted.

Introduction

During a meeting with a British film-maker in 2012, Christian Prudhomme, the sixth and current director of the Tour de France, threw up his hands and said: 'You have won.'

Prudhomme had been asked if he spoke English. 'You used to have to speak French,' he joked. 'But now it is us who have to speak English.'

Perhaps he was exaggerating, a little. But Prudhomme's comments hinted at one significant change in the Tour de France over the 100 editions of the great race, since the first one set off from the Café au Reveil Matin, on the outskirts of Paris, on 1 July 1903. It was, from the beginning, resolutely French. As French as a bicycle-riding Frenchman wearing a beret and a string of onions.

As French as … well, as the Tour de France.

Even in the 1920s, when Paris was the hub of an extraordinary English-speaking literary scene, there was one increasingly significant feature of French cultural life that seemed tantalisingly out-of-reach. F. Scott Fitzgerald, James Joyce, Ernest Hemingway and, a little later, Samuel Beckett addressed many aspects of life in France, but none would, or could, write about the Tour de France. (Though it was rumoured that a source of inspiration for Beckett's play, *Waiting for Godot*, was a French cyclist called Godot, the last man, or 'lanterne rouge', in one Tour.)

Typically, it was Hemingway who directly addressed the subject. Or, rather, he addressed the dilemma facing English-language writers. 'I must write the strange world of the six-day races and the marvels of the road-racing in the mountains,' said Hemingway in *A Moveable Feast*, his memoir of life in Paris. 'French is the only language it has ever been written in properly and the terms are all French and that is what makes it so hard to write.'

The language of the Tour, and indeed of the sport, was always French. It is only in the past three decades that this began to change, slowly at first, then accelerating in the Lance Armstrong era (1999–2005). But this is no incidental

L'Auto

AUTOMOBILE — CYCLISME

ATHLÉTISME, YACHTING, AÉROSTATION, ESCRIME, POIDS et HALTÈRES, HIPPISME, GYMNASTIQUE, ALPINISME

Directeur-Rédacteur en Chef : HENRI DESGRANGE

LE TOUR DE FRANCE — LE DÉPART

Organisé par L'AUTO du 1er au 19 Juillet 1903

LA SEMENCE

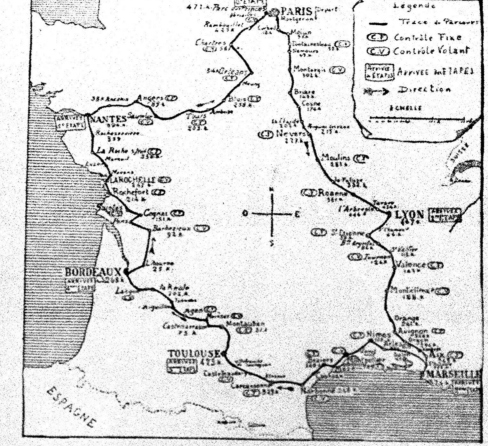

L'ITINÉRAIRE DU TOUR DE FRANCE

QUI ?

Maurice GARIN

Father of the Tour ▶

Henri Desgrange had been a racing cyclist before becoming a journalist with *L'Auto* and the first organiser of the Tour. This despite fearing for its future as early as the second race, writing: 'The Tour de France is finished and the second edition will, I fear, also be the last. It has died of its success, of the blind passions that it unleashed, the abuse and the dirty suspicions.' Here he is towards the end of his 33-year reign, in 1932, alongside the Italian *touriste-routier* Amerigo Caccioni in Montpellier, before stage eight.

point. Language – words – have always been an absolutely vital element to the great race: a point emphasised by the fact that it was set up by a newspaper, *L'Auto*, and, moreover, conceived as a way of increasing sales of the newspaper (which later became the sports daily *L'Equipe*).

Just as the newspaper needed the Tour, so the Tour needed newspapers. Here was a sport that didn't take place in a conventional arena, before the eyes of fans and reporters; it happened on the open road, in the wilderness and the mountains, largely out of view. The upshot was that nobody – not even the riders – really knew what was going on; they saw only glimpses and snapshots, never the full picture. And so it represented an interesting but exciting challenge to those who chronicled it – often in flowery, highly descriptive (French) language, and with considerably more artistic licence (not to mention vivid imaginations) than writers could get away with if they were describing a football or tennis match, or an athletics meeting.

It started, then, with the written word, with radio entering the fray in 1930, and television coming along in 1948, when French TV made its first ever external live broadcast from the finish in Paris.

But as well as the written word there was, from the beginning, another means

of capturing 'the marvels of the road-racing in the mountains': photography. Even if the language has changed over the years, with the reporting becoming less imaginative as the TV cameras' lenses leave less to the imagination, photography has been the one constant medium through which the sport has been best captured in all its glory, and gory. Indeed, for many it is photography that remains the ultimate medium; the one that best conveys the epic scale, the stunning scenery, the pain and suffering, the drama and excitement, and, most of all, the sheer beauty of the Tour de France.

Photographers have a special role at the Tour, and they enjoy certain privileges. For one thing, they do not stand apart from the action in order to passively observe it; they are in it. Whereas at football and tennis matches, or at athletics tracks, the 'field of play' is sacrosanct, with entry to non-players forbidden, at the Tour there are no white lines, no firm boundaries. The motorbike-mounted photographers effectively share the road – the playing field – with the riders. That means they share some of the dangers, too. It also means that a bond is forged between them.

The riders have to trust the photographers, and not merely to take nice pictures. Though this, too, is important in such a visual sport, which has always attached a high value to aesthetics, and which at one point awarded a prize to the 'most elegant rider.' Some riders were more aware of their appearance than others. The Swiss star of the 1950s, Hugo Koblet, used to carry a bottle of eau de cologne and a comb in the rear pocket of his jersey to spruce up for the finish, and the photographs.

* * * * * * * *

The Tour is now a global event, regularly described as the world's biggest annual sporting event, but it was conceived over coffee in a brasserie in Montmartre on 20 November 1902.

On a spring day in 2012 I paid a visit to the Boulevard Montmartre, to try and find the Taverne Zimmer (referred to in some places as the Zimmer Madrid restaurant), where two journalists and an accountant from the newspaper *L'Auto* first discussed the idea. It followed a brainstorming session (which wouldn't, of course, have been described as such) in the offices of the paper, around the corner on the Rue du Faubourg. Géo Lefevre, a young journalist, suggested a race around France as a way of saving *L'Auto*, the upstart newspaper that was struggling to compete against its mighty rival, *Le Vélo*. Lefevre's boss, Henri Desgrange, responded: 'If I understand you right, petit Géo, what you are proposing is a Tour de France?'

Around the corner to the Zimmer they went – Desgrange, Lefevre and the paper's accountant, Victor Goddet – to discuss the proposal. They didn't get around to that until the coffees arrived. And there they agreed: they would organise a cycle race around France, trumping, at least in scale, the most prestigious road races of the day, all of them one-day events. Multi-day races were held, but on the track, not the road. The Tour de France combined the best elements of both disciplines: the multi-day format of the track and the epic scale and challenges of long-distance road racing. It was simple but ingenious.

Today, there is no sign of the Taverne Zimmer. Nor is there any indication of where it might have been, or that the Tour de France was effectively born there. But in a small close off the boulevard, the Passages des Panoramas, in a shop selling antique postcards and pictures, I asked the proprietor if he could help. '*Bien sûr*,' he replied, disappearing into the back of the shop. A moment later he reappeared with a 1906 phone directory. '*Voila!*' He leafed through its thin, yellowing, crispy pages, eventually finding the Zimmer: it occupied number 18. Today, it is called the Indiana Cafe; but the waiter I spoke to had no idea of its links to the great bike race.

On the day of stage one of the first Tour, starting at 3.16pm on 1 July 1903, from the Café au Reveil Matin, on the outskirts of Paris (which is still there, with a commemorative plaque), *L'Auto* published its mission statement, penned by Desgrange:

'With the broad and powerful swing of the hand which Zola in *The Earth* gave to his ploughman, *L'Auto*, journal of ideas and action, is going to fling across France today those reckless and uncouth sowers of energy who are the great professional riders of the world … From Paris to the blue waves of the Mediterranean, from Marseille to Bordeaux, passing along the roseate

and dreaming roads sleeping under the sun, across the calm of the fields of the Vendée, following the Loire, which flows on still and silent, our men are going to race madly, unflaggingly.'

The Tour did save *L'Auto*. Sales jumped from 25,000 to 65,000 as the first race wound around France, and the country's top cyclist, Maurice Garin, lived up to his billing as favourite by leading from start to finish. The general classification that first year was decided by accumulated time. It was changed in 1904 to a points-based system, rewarding the most consistent daily finisher, and changed back in 1913 (permanently) to a time-based classification. Garin won again in 1904, only to be one of several riders disqualified by the world governing body after an investigation into various forms of alleged cheating: short cuts, holding on to cars, train rides, tacks on the road. So dispirited by this was Desgrange that he declared the second Tour to have been the last: 'It has died of its success, of the blind passions that it unleashed, the abuse and the dirty suspicions …'

Plus ça change, plus c'est la même chose. One hundred Tours later, it still unleashes blind passions and is regularly engulfed in dirty suspicions.

The Tour these days may seem unrecognisable from the early Tours in which riders struggled over dirt roads, spare tyres wrapped around their bodies, finishing with grime-encrusted faces, as though they had emerged from a coal mine. And yet, as I read the history, and delved in the photographic archives, I was struck by how similar it is. The bikes have improved, of course, but they haven't really changed. It is a team sport these days; but there was always, much to Desgrange's chagrin, a significant team element, and, very quickly, a clear hierarchy, with domestiques (team helpers) devoted to helping a designated leader. Another crucial element of the Tour, as Desgrange acknowledged in his mission statement, was that it involved professional riders. While other sports – notably the modern Olympics, founded by another Frenchman – cherished amateurism and held those ideals firm, the Tour was never so idealistic. While in the early days the idea of 'professionalism' saw the riders have the status of manual workers (Tour riders were called *ouvriers de la pedale* – workers of the pedal), plying their trade in what was a decidedly working-class sport, from the 1950s onwards the best came to be recognised, instead, as stars; a process that reached its apotheosis with Lance Armstrong, the cancer-beating, seven-Tours-de-France winning, global icon, before he was revealed as a drugs cheat and stripped of those titles.

What has changed most – apart from the surprising fact that today's stages are much shorter than in the early races – is the media coverage. The Tour is broadcast in close to 200 countries and covered by 2,500 journalists, including almost 300 photographers. But another change is in the role of newspapers in the race. It is ironic to note that an event conceived to sell newspapers may actually outlive newspapers: a case of the marketing trick outliving the market.

This book contains a mixture of pictures and words arranged in chapters tied to particular eras. The pictures speak for themselves, though the captions should help identify the particular *ouvriers de la pedale* and put them in context. Please don't let the fact that those words are in English put you off.

Goddet and the first Tour super-champ

Jacques Goddet, who succeeded Henri Desgrange in 1936 and served as Tour director for fifty years, with the first five-time winner, Jacques Anquetil, in 1963.

Today's man in charge ▲

Christian Prudhomme took over from Jean-Marie Leblanc in 2006, continuing the tradition for journalists to run the Tour de France. Here he is with Fabian Cancellara, in the yellow jersey, during the 2012 race.

'Murderers!' Octave Lapize yelled at the Tour organisers at the summit of the
Col d'Aubisque in 1910. The Aubisque was the day's sixth of seven mountains.
Here he is close to the summit of the third and highest, the 2,115m Col du
Tourmalet. Lapize would eventually be crowned winner in Paris. It was the
only Tour he ever finished.

The circle of death, 1903–14

The tenth stage of the 1910 Tour de France began at 2am on 21 July. They left
Luchon to ride 326km to Bayonne. Neither the distance nor the start time was
unusual. And nor was the fact that the following day was a rest day: the riders
'only' raced every second day from 1903 to 1924. It was the only way the late
finishers could get enough rest before they got back on their bikes.

What was unusual was that, for the first time in the Tour's eight-year history,
they were in the Pyrenees. The ghostly, cone-shaped silhouettes that could
be discerned in the 2am gloom, from Luchon's Allées d'Étigny, were of the
mountain range that sits on the French-Spanish border. The previous stage had
been a taster, with four climbs. But today was a monster, with almost twice as
many mountains; and mountains that were almost twice as high.

In the 21st century, three or four such climbs would be considered a major
mountain stage. If, in addition, the distance were more than 200km, it would be
described as brutal. But in 1910 they were sent out to tackle seven – seven! On
the itinerary were the Col de Peyresourde, Col d'Aspin, Col du Tourmalet, Col du
Soulour, Col de Tortes, Col d'Aubisque, and finally the Col d'Osquich. The Col de
Tortes last featured in the Tour in 1940; the truth is, none of these passes would
feature in any road book now; or not as anything more sophisticated than a
goat track.

Octave Lapize was a five-foot-five, curly-headed all-rounder, as adept on the
track as he was on the roads – or goat tracks – of the Tour de France. But he
didn't really know what he was getting himself into when he set off from
Luchon, and neither did most of the others. One hundred and thirty-six riders
had entered the Tour, though 26 pulled out before it even started, when they
heard the route would include such high mountains. After nine stages, there
were 59 left as the race prepared for the Pyrenees.

Of Lapize's rivals, some had conducted their own pre-Tour 'recce'. Lucien Petit-
Breton, the winner in 1907, had been to the south-west of France and ridden
the roads, and declared himself horrified. The riders, he said, would be entering
'the circle of death'. It wasn't just the gradients or the rough tracks; Petit-Breton

The little chimney sweep

Maurice Garin, the pre-race favourite and winner of the first Tour de France in 1903. 'The Little Chimney Sweep', as he was known, won in 1904 as well but was later disqualified, along with the other three riders in the top four, for cheating. It had been rife, with riders holding on to vehicles, even catching trains, and, much later, from the petrol station he had opened with his prize money from the second Tour (which he never returned), Garin said that he had done it because everybody else was cheating. He made a comeback to ride the 1911 Tour before retiring.

was also concerned that bears stalked the upper reaches. The cyclists would be easy prey.

In fact, the 1910 Tour was the first to suffer a fatality, but it didn't happen in this circle of death. It was in Nice, on the rest day following stage six, when Adolphe Hélière went for a swim. The cause of death was said to be a jellyfish sting.

That was an unforeseen and avoidable tragedy. But what of the Pyrenees? Was the stage a greater tragedy waiting to happen? What were the organisers thinking of? Henri Desgrange, the Tour's founding father and director, was said to be torn, as the race prepared to enter the high mountains, on the wisdom of this initiative. Six months before the Grand Départ he had sent his course designer, Alphones Steinès, to check their suitability.

It was in the depths of January that Steinès ventured out, ignoring the advice of a local innkeeper, driving his rented car over the highest road in the Pyrenees, up the Tourmalet. The snow was heavy at the bottom, and it thickened all the way up, until he could drive no further. Steinès abandoned his car and walked to the summit, upon which he became disoriented, and, as night began to close, fell into a ravine. At 3am he was discovered by a search party. The next morning, he sent a telegram to Desgrange: 'Have crossed the Tourmalet on foot stop Road passable to vehicles stop No snow stop.'

It was unambiguous, and, of course, inexplicable. Perhaps the cold had addled Steinès' brain. And perhaps Desgrange was suspicious of the gung-ho attitude of his course designer, because, after witnessing the first, moderately difficult day in the Pyrenees, he fled to Paris, leaving his deputy, Victor Breyer, in charge. The official reason for his sudden disappearance was that Desgrange was feeling off-colour. Others suggested that he was afraid of the damage about to be inflicted on the race – and the riders. Alternatively, in the opinion of Jean Bobin, Lapize's biographer, his abandonment might even have resulted from his disappointment at so many riders finishing the previous day's stage. 'I would say that Desgrange was in a pretty bad mood,' Bobet conjectured. 'For him, it was intolerable that 59 of the 62 riders who left Perpignan had made it to Luchon. Steines reassured him, predicting a 50 per cent wastage between Luchon and Bayonne.'

'Wastage' – it's an evocative word. And it cuts to the heart of Desgrange's original conception of the Tour de France, and, indeed, his motivation for wishing to include the Pyrenees in the first place. For Desgrange, the Tour was supposed to be a war of attrition, a battle for survival; in his ideal scenario, only one man would make it to the finish in Paris.

Yet Bobet suggests that Desgrange was himself divided over the wisdom of including the Pyrenees. While the devil on one shoulder encouraged him to seek out ever more inhumane challenges, the angel urged caution. 'Some of the more mischievous observers claimed that Desgrange was scared of losing the

Tour on the Tourmalet,' said Bobet. Whether it was the roads and the conditions he most feared, or the bears, he does not say …

At the summit of the Peyresourde, after 15km of climbing, Gustave Garrigou and Lapize led, with the others scattered behind; their closest pursuers were already four minutes down. At the top of the Aspin, Lapize was three minutes clear of Garrigou, though he was caught on the descent. On the 'Queen of the Pyrenees,' the Tourmalet, their battle – as well as the race itself – reached its apotheosis. About halfway up, Lapize surged ahead, but then he dismounted. The gear he used was, by today's standards, enormous; he and Garrigou were struggling to keep the pedals turning, though Garrigou managed to ride all the way to the summit, as Lapize conceded defeat and wheeled his bike up the mountain. But it was Lapize who, by this unconventional method, reached the summit first. For doing so, he collected a 100-franc bonus. It was 7.30am: he had been riding for five hours.

On they went. But at the summit of the penultimate mountain, the Aubisque, the man deputising for Desgrange, Victor Breyer, dared to ask Lapize, who had fallen 15 minutes behind a local rider, François Lafourcade, if he was alright. Lapize rolled his eyes. 'What's wrong? Breyer inquired.

'You're murderers!' responded Lapize. 'That's what's wrong! You're criminals!'

Over the remaining 180km Lapize caught the escapee and won the sprint in Bayonne at 5.40pm to claim the stage after 14 hours, 2 minutes. Some of Lapize's rivals were still 90km away in Mauleon.

That night, Breyer also stood in for Desgrange in chronicling the day's events in L'Auto. He could barely contain his glee as he wrote that, at the finish, 'the riders were drunk with fatigue, the race followers with the day's images, and the spectators with delight ... It's improbable! It's madness! It's unheard of! It's everything you could wish for!'

Lapize went on to win the Tour for the first and only time. Seven years and one week later, as a fighter pilot in the French army during the First World War, he was shot down and killed.

At the finish in Paris, in 1910, Desgrange seemed happy – to a point. 'There could be many reasons for me to take pleasure in the success of this eighth Tour de France,' he wrote in L'Auto, 'but first of all there is a fact we must face: we brought far too many people to Paris, and there was not enough wastage … Out of 110 starters, 41 riders finished the race. I repeat that this is far too many. The Tour de France has a reputation for being an extremely tough event; let us justify public opinion by putting new obstacles in front of our men.'

The next year, he added the Alps.

L'arrivée
Louis Trousselier, the winner of the 1905 Tour, arriving at the finish in Paris. He gambled away all his winnings that night in a game of dice with friends.

A broken heart
One of the Tour's first – but certainly not the last – tragic figures, René Pottier won the 1906 Tour, which included the mountains of the Massif Central. But his heartbreak over an ended love affair led 27-year old Pottier to hang himself just six months after his success. When he was found his medals and trophies were neatly arranged at his feet.

War of attrition ▶
The Tour made its first visit to the high
mountains of the Pyrenees in 1910, in a
bid to toughen up the race and fulfil Henri
Desgrange's ambition of having only one
rider survive to the finish in Paris.

A petit double ▶

The first double winner, after Maurice Garin was stripped of his second Tour, Petit-Breton was a member of the powerful Peugeot team. He won in 1907 and 1908, when he also claimed five of the 14 stages. Like Octave Lapize and François Faber, the 1908 runner-up, Petit-Breton was a casualty of the First World War, dying when he crashed into an oncoming vehicle near the front in Troyes in December 1917.

▲ **A giant of the road**

François Faber runs towards victory in the 1909 Tour. The Luxembourger was
the first non-French winner, but was raised in Paris and known as the Giant of
Colombes: he was over 6 foot, and 200 pounds. Despite his size he was named
by *L'Auto* as *meilleur grimpeur* (best climber). He was killed during the First World
War after bravely attempting to rescue an injured colleague from no-man's land.

Le Frisé

Known as 'Le Frisé' for his curly hair,
Octave Lapize was one of the leading
riders of the era, on road and track, but he
made a habit of abandoning the Tour de
France, much to the annoyance of Henri
Desgrange. He only finished it once, in
1910, but he did so as the race winner.

The first champion

Maurice Garin enters the Longchamp circuit in Paris at the finish of the final stage of the first Tour. This gave him his third stage win – of the six that made up the race – as he won by 2 hours, 59 minutes, 31 seconds: still the greatest ever winning margin.

France en fête
It didn't take long for the Tour to capture the public imagination. Here crowds
await stage two of the first race, from Lyon to Marseille.

Into the mountains ▶

Without the low gears that later bikes would have, most of the riders ended up pushing their bikes for some way up the big climbs. Here Octave Lapize nears the summit of the highest point of the 1910 Tour, the Col du Tourmalet, surrounded by fans who seem curiously indifferent to the eventual winner.

▼ Long shadows

Octave Lapize tackles the Col d'Aspin in 1910, the second of seven Pyrenean climbs on the 326km tenth stage. The length of Lapize's shadow, as it stretches out in front of him, indicates the earliness of the hour.

Into the darkness ▲
They started at 2am, when the Pyrenees were shrouded in darkness: Lapize pushes his bike up the Col de Peyresourde, helped by the headlights of the following car.

Foul play

The 1911 winner was Gustave Garrigou, a strong climber who benefited from the addition of the Alps. But his victory was controversial. His French rival Paul Duboc was allegedly given a bottle containing a poisonous liquid at a feeding station in the Pyrenees, and promptly began vomiting – which saved his life. Many believed Garrigou to be behind the episode.

Goat tracks

The great Eugène Christophe in the Alps during the 1912 Tour. Christophe rode his first Tour in 1906 and his last in 1925, aged 40. He never won, and suffered atrocious luck, but he claimed three stage victories, all in 1912, including the stage to Grenoble after the longest ever solo break: 315 km.

Hairpin hell ▲
Jean Alavoine and Firmin Lambot climb the
Alpine monster, the Col du Galibier, during
the 1913 Tour.

Running on dynamite ▶

Henri Pélissier, his brother Francis and Maurice Ville, speak to the reporter Albert Londres after withdrawing from the race in protest at Henri Desgrange's arcane clothing regulations, in 1924. 'We run on dynamite,' Francis told Londres after showing him the drugs they were using.

The yellow jersey, 1919–29

When the Tour de France restarted after the war, in 1919, it did so with a field of just 65 riders. This owed something to the devastation of the Great War: Lucien Petit-Breton, the winner in 1907 and '08, François Faber, the champion in 1909, and Octave Lapize, who triumphed in 1910, were among those who died in action. What's more, when the Tour restarted, only 11 riders made it back to the finish in Paris. It was the kind of 'wastage' of which Henri Desgrange might have approved.

But one significant piece of history was made in 1919: it was the first Tour to feature a yellow jersey. And the first man to wear it was Eugène Christophe. Christophe was one of the great survivors, his most famous escapade having come in 1913, when, on the stage from Bayonne to Luchon, as he began to climb the Col du Tourmalet, he was hit by one of the Tour's following cars, causing the forks holding his front wheel to break.

Christophe walked 10km to the nearest village, Ste Marie-de-Campan, where he met a young girl who pointed him towards a local blacksmith's. These days, a convoy of support vehicles follows the Tour; if a rider has the kind of mechanical mishap Christophe suffered, he is given a spare bike and is usually back in the race within minutes. Back then, however, the rules not only disallowed spare bikes, they insisted that riders carry out repairs themselves, with no outside help.

Countless riders suffered as a consequence, but Christophe's story became the most famous: while he welded his forks back together, refusing the offer of help from the blacksmith, a seven-year-old boy worked the bellows to keep the fire going. That external 'help' earned Christophe a ten-minute penalty.

In 1919 it happened again, at a point when he was leading by 28 minutes; he eventually finished third in Paris, having suffered a record number of punctures on the final day. (*L'Auto* organised a collection for the Tour's most unlucky rider, which raised 13,310 francs, trumping what Christophe would have taken home as winner.)

By then, Christophe had also been presented with the first maillot jaune (yellow

Three times unlucky ▶
A picture that could sum up the career of the hapless, hugely unlucky, and enormously popular Eugène Christophe. On three occasions Christophe suffered broken forks, forcing him to walk for miles to find a blacksmith's forge and carry out the repairs himself – as Henri Desgrange's rules stipulated.

jersey), inspired, according to legend, by the yellow pages of the Tour's founding newsaper, *L'Auto*. An alternative theory has it that one of the team managers, the formidable Alphonse Baugé, complained to Desgrange that the riders all looked the same in their grey shirts; the war had ended only seven months earlier and the clothing manufacturer, La Sportive, had only been able to source grey wool.

Desgrange responded to Baugé's complaint by introducing a special leader's jersey, in yellow. But 40 years later, Philippe Thys, the first triple winner, claimed that Desgrange had urged him to wear a yellow jersey while leading the 1913 Tour, and that he had refused because he didn't want to stand out. He was forced to wear it by Desgrange, he said; though the Tour's official history is unsure about the veracity of Thys's story.

Six years later, Desgrange presented Christophe with his yellow jersey before the start of stage 11, though he had been leading since stage four. Christophe didn't like it; he complained that he was ridiculed by his peers, who said he looked like 'a canary.'

Not that he would have been happy to lose it two days later, when, on the mammoth 468km stage from Metz to Dunkirk, it happened again – his forks broke. And exactly the same thing happened for a third time in 1922, while Christophe was descending the Col du Galibier. Once again he found a blacksmith's and carried out the repairs before continuing. 'That accident didn't upset me as much as the others,' he later reflected. 'By then I was a bit of an expert.'

On each occasion the mechanical failure might have cost Christophe the victory; he rode 11 Tours, finishing eight, but he never did win. Desgrange's strict rules were not restricted to roadside repairs. Others included

that riders had to finish with what they started, including clothing. Even if the temperature soared in the south of France, or plummeted in the mountains, they could remove or add layers, but had to finish with what they started. At one point in the mid-1920s Desgrange was keen to introduce a similar rule with food: he wanted them all to eat the same, in the same quantities. When he tried to impose that one, the riders – led by 1923 winner Henri Pélissier – objected. Unusually, Desgrange relented.

It is not difficult to imagine Desgrange's motivations, even if many of his rules appear draconian (he also outlawed derailleur gears when they first appeared). But some of them, particularly with regard to equipment, are at the heart of cycling's traditional and enduring appeal.

Even today, the riders of the Tour compete on 'standard' bikes – there are weight restrictions and other rules imposed by the world governing body, the UCI, intended to ensure that the sport remains primarily a contest between men rather than machines. This helps explain why modern bikes are essentially the same as those ridden by Tour cyclists in the early 20th century: the diamond-shaped frame, with similar diameters, size of wheels, and all-too-fallible tyres and tubes. The materials have changed, and there have been major innovations in gears and pedals, for example, but the bikes are recognisable in a way that Formula One cars, for example, are not. And therein lies the cautionary tale: while F1 can appear to celebrate the car over the driver, at the Tour it is still – to paraphrase the title of Lance Armstrong's best-selling autobiography – not all about the bike. Perhaps we have Desgrange to thank for that.

But some of his regulations – including the clothing rule – put him in opposition to certain of the riders, especially the combative Henri Pélissier, the

1923 winner. The following year tension between Desgrange and Pélissier flared when, in Cherbourg, on a cold stage early in the Tour, the bold Pélissier was approached by a commissaire (referee), who wanted to carry out a clothing check, in order to ensure, later, that nothing had been discarded. Pélissier was furious and went to find Desgrange, asking him: 'I haven't got the right to throw my jersey on the road, then?'

'No,' said Desgrange, 'you can't throw away Tour property.'

'It's not Tour property, it's mine.'

'I will not hold discussions in the street,' said Desgrange, adding that they would talk about it at the finish in Brest. But on the stage, as the temperature rose, Pélissier defied Desgrange, removing one of his two jerseys and tossing it away. Desgrange was incandescent; Pélissier was unrepentant. He went and found his brother, Francis, and a third rider, Maurice Ville, and together they withdrew from the race and decamped to a bar in Coutances. There, they attracted an even bigger crowd than the race itself.

One of France's most distinguished journalists, Albert Londres of *Le Petit Parisien*, joined this crowd as Henri held court with the meeting between Londres and the riders captured in an evocative picture (page 29). 'We're not dogs,' said Pélissier, as Londres scribbled in his notebook.

'It's not enough that we should race like brutes, we also have to freeze or stifle as well,' Henri continued. 'You have no idea what the Tour de France is. It's a calvary. And what's more, the way to the cross only had 14 stations — we've got 15.' Henri then offered to show Londres 'how we keep going', pulling phials and containers from his bag. 'That's cocaine for our eyes, and chloroform for our gums,' he said. Ville joined in: 'That's horse ointment to warm my knees.' Then they produced boxes of pills. 'We run on dynamite,' explained Francis.

'My name is Pélissier,' added Henri after he had finished describing the brutality of it all, 'not Atlas.' Convinced by all this, Londres coined the term *les forçats de la route* (the convicts of the road) to describe the riders. The Tour cyclist was also known as '*ouvrir de la pedale*' (pedal workers): an interesting and significant description, given its connotations – of which Desgrange would have approved – of the cyclist as worker. It wasn't until the 1950s that they became recognised, instead, as stars. But this may be why Henri Pélissier rubbed Desgrange up the wrong way; he was a star, so popular that, the day after his win in the 1923 Tour, sales of *L'Auto* surged from 600,000 to a million.

In the Pélissier brothers' absence, the 1924 Tour was won by Ottavio Bottecchia, who had been encouraged to ride in France in 1923 by none other than Henri Pélissier himself. In his first year, Bottecchia helped Pélissier win; the next year he became the first Italian winner, as well as the first man ever to lead the Tour from start to finish; and in 1924 he won again. But that was to be it for Bottecchia, whose story, already extraordinary – he had been an illiterate bricklayer who became a decorated fighter in the war, then a cyclist – was about to take a tragic twist.
In 1926, in atrocious weather in the Pyrenees, Bottecchia withdrew in tears

while his domestique, Lucien Buysse, went on to inherit his title, just as he had succeeded his old mentor. Bottecchia, whose swept-back dark hair, gaunt appearance and sharp cheekbones meant he bore a resemblance to Fausto Coppi, the Italian Campionissimo who would emerge two decades later, was by now famous, feted in France and Italy. But he wasn't an uncontroversial figure. Having learned to read, he became interested in anti-fascist, anti-Mussolini literature, a possible reason for his decision, on stage nine of the 1924 race, from Toulon to Nice, to opt for team colours rather than the yellow jersey. As the Tour passed close to Italy, he might have been worried about attracting the attention of Mussolini supporters – wearing his team jersey allowed him to be incognito.

It is a theory that might also tie in to his tragic death. On 3 June 1927, Bottecchia woke at dawn in his home in Peonis, north-east Italy, and asked his wife to prepare a hot bath for his return, in three hours, from his training ride. He called on his friend and training partner, Alfonso Piccini, who declined to join him; then he tried to rope in Riccardo Zille, though he too was unable to join Bottechia. And so he set off alone.

A couple of hours later he was discovered lying by the roadside, close to Peonis. He had a cracked skull and other broken bones. His bike lay on the verge, unmarked. Indeed, other than his injuries, there was no evidence that he had crashed. He was carried to a bar and given the last rites by a priest, then taken by cart to a hospital, where he died twelve days later.

The mystery of Bottecchia's death has never been solved. Did he suffer sunstroke and collapse? Was he killed by fascists? The plot thickened when, years later, an Italian man in New York, who lay dying after being stabbed, owned up to Bottecchia's murder. He claimed he'd been hired as a hit man by a local godfather. But there followed another deathbed confession: a farmer said that he'd caught Bottecchia eating grapes in his vineyard and thrown a rock that hit his head.

Bottecchia was not the last great Italian cyclist to meet an early and controversial death – see also Fausto Coppi and Marco Pantani – and nor was he the only rider of his era to suffer such a fate.

Henri Pélissier's death, eleven years after his spat with Desgrange, is not shrouded in mystery, but it is no less shocking. His first wife, Léonie, shot herself in 1933, following which Henri got together with a younger woman, Camille Tharault. His violent behaviour towards her included threatening her with a knife during a row in their home near Paris on 1 May 1935. Tharault escaped to the bedroom, retrieved the gun that Pélissier's wife had used to kill herself, and returned to the kitchen. As Pélissier lunged at her with the knife, she shot him five times. She was given a year's suspended prison sentence.

Ironically, a happier fate awaited the man who never won the Tour, Eugène Christophe, who began racing in 1904 and retired in 1926. Christophe lived to the age of 85. And hanging in his workshop in his home in Malakoff, where he lived all his life, were the forks he had broken, and repaired, in Ste Marie-de-Campan in 1913.

▲ **Tour reborn**
Firmin Lambot of Belgium after the first of his two Tour wins in 1919, as the race
stuttered back into life after the First World War. Only 11 riders made it to Paris,
and most believed Eugène Christophe would have won had he not broken the
forks of his bike – as he also did in 1913, and would do again in 1922.

Italian double ▶
Ottavio Bottecchia, the first Italian winner of the Tour, in 1924. He won again in 1925 and died in mysterious circumstances two years later.

◀ **Riding on anger**
Belgian riders Louis Mottiat and Léon Scieur struggle up the majestic Col du Galibier on stage 10 of the 1921 Tour, from Nice to Grenoble. Scieur was riding on anger. He punctured on the stage and another Belgian, Hector Heusghem, broke the unwritten rule by attacking him. Scieur repaired his puncture, caught Heusghem, reprimanded him, took off and won in Grenoble.

▲ **The peloton crosses the pont**
Sailors watching the Tour de France at the port of Roquefort during the sixth
stage of the 1925 race, won by the eventual champion, Ottavio Bottecchia.

The first domestique?

Lucien Buysse leads eventual winner Ottavio Bottecchia through Saint-Cloud on the final stage of the 1925 Tour. Buysse had acted as Bottecchia's faithful domestique during that Tour but still finished second to the Italian. He had his chance the next year, and took it, winning overall. The term 'domestique' was first coined by Henri Desgrange to describe Maurice Brocco, for his work on behalf of François Faber in the 1911 Tour. Writing in *L'Auto*, Desgrange said of Brocco: 'He is unworthy. He is no more than a domestique.'

▲ **All lined out**
The peloton races through the Ardennes town of Sedan, in the north-east of
France, during the 1927 Tour. The high speed is indicated by the fact that the
riders are in single file, the peloton stretched in a long line.

Tour de Frantz ▶
Luxembourg rider Nicolas Frantz celebrates his second consecutive Tour win in 1928. By all accounts Frantz was one of the less colourful champions, most often described as 'taciturn.' It is a rare image that catches him smiling.

◄ **Team work**

The riders await the start of the 1929 Tour. Maurice De Waele became the fifth Belgian winner, even though he crashed frequently and was sick. His victory owed rather more to his team, the powerful Alcyon squad, than Henri Desgrange, the organiser, would have liked. 'My Tour has been won by a corpse,' he complained. The next year he banned professional teams and invited national teams instead.

Thys a winner

Philippe Thys, the first three-time winner of the Tour (1913, 1914, 1921), leads the peloton during the 1924 race, on the road to Bayonne.

Running repairs ▶

Firmin Lambot jumping back on his bike after carrying out repairs during the 1920 Tour, in which he finished third behind his fellow Belgian, the three-time winner Philippe Thys. Incredibly, Belgians filled the first seven places in this Tour. They also won 12 of the 15 stages

▼ **Out of the saddle**

A spectacular image of Firmin Lambot on the switchbacks of the Col du Galibier, 1920.

A complicated business

Ottavio Bottecchia, the 1924 and '25 winner, fixing a puncture during the 1924 race while a spectator, holding a baby, looks on. Even had she wanted to help, the rules precluded outside assistance. Fixing a puncture was a complicated business: the stitching holding the base of the tyre had to be cut, then the inner tube repaired, before the tyre could be sewn back together.

▲ **Allez Ottavio**
Bottecchia on the Tourmalet on his way to victory in 1924.

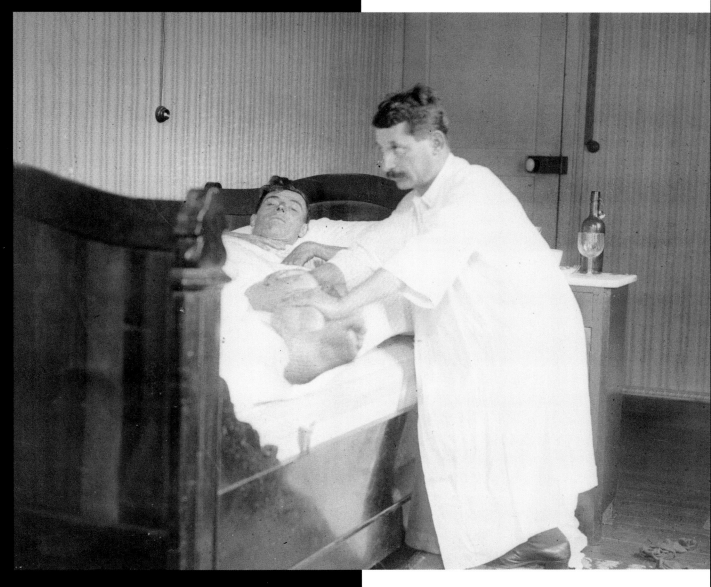

Healing hands ▼

'Soigneurs' were already present on the
Tour. Their jobs included massage and
looking after their riders' health and
well-being. Later, some would acquire a
reputation for shady practices, including
doping. Here, Ottavio Bottecchia's
soigneur rubs life back into his legs
during the 1924 race.

Pressure on ▲
Henri Pélissier, Maurice Ville and Robert Jacquinot lead the peloton by the French coast during the 1924 Tour. Racing conditions are often difficult on coastal roads, due to the strong winds. The lined-out nature of the peloton suggests the pressure is on.

◄ **Camera, action**
Francis Pélissier leads the bunch through packed, narrow streets on stage 12 of the 1923 Tour, from Strasbourg to Geneva and appears to be posing for the camera to his right.

One of the Tour's iconic images: René Vietto waits at the roadside in tears having given his front wheel to his team leader, Antonin Magne. His sacrifice provided one of the earliest and, thanks to the presence of a photographer, most poignant illustrations of the role of the domestique (team helper).

Giants of the road, 1930–47

The 1930s saw huge changes to the Tour. It was the decade in which some aspects of the modern Tour were introduced: 1934 saw the first time trial, and the first 'split-stage,' which actually meant two in a day. Another initiative was the publicity caravan, which came along in 1935, apparently as garish, tacky and tasteless – yet hugely popular with the roadside fans – as it remains today.

The *caravane publicitaire* was at least true to the Tour's commercial roots. It travelled along the route two hours before the riders and comprised vehicles advertising all manner of consumables, and dishing out thousands of freebies to spectators, with adults turning into children in the stampede – a phenomenon that can still be witnessed today.

As Les Woodland explained in his book, *The Unknown Tour de France*, the value of the publicity caravan arguably peaked in the 1930s, 'before advertising on television and before continuous live coverage of the Tour. Then, a crowd of hundreds of thousands all around France was an irresistible target for a marketing man and companies competed to attract most attention, to come up with the most original and striking ideas.'

Not everyone approved. The journalist Pierre Bost, during that 1935 Tour, wrote that advertising in general, and the publicity caravan in particular, 'mushrooms around the whole spectacle', and is 'not very glorious. The caravan of 60 vividly painted trucks extolling the virtues of an aperitif, or of underwear, or rubbish bins, presents a shameful sight. It shouts, it plays bad music, it's ugly, it's sad, it's horrible – it's the vulgarity of money.'

Another 1930s initiative changed the character of the Tour for the next 30 years: Henri Desgrange insisted on national teams rather than the professional 'trade' teams that had previously entered and, in his view, distorted the race with their unofficial collaborations and underhand shenanigans. National teams would, he reasoned, restore some purity to the race. Other 1930s Desgrange regulations included the issuing of standard bikes, though he did eventually relent and allow riders to fit their own saddles. This didn't go down well with bike manufactures, obviously, and they – and their commercial interests – eventually won the day.

< **The Monk**
Antonin Magne, nicknamed 'The Monk', in action during the 1930 Tour. He would go on to win the race in 1931 and '34, and then to a career as one of the most formidable team *directeurs sportifs* in cycling history.

By the 1930s the Tour was firmly established as a national event. But it was more than a sporting event; it was a cultural one, too, of huge significance to France and the French people. Still at the helm were Desgrange and *L'Auto*, and the Tour had achieved more than they could have dreamt of. Daily sales of the paper climbed to 800,000 in the middle part of the decade. The event could also be said to have contributed to France's sense of itself, not least in educating its own people on the wonders of a country that, according to the Tour's preferred narrative, was simultaneously diverse and united; an idea that both symbolised and was perhaps reinforced by the Tour.

Breathless reports in *L'Auto* spoke of the French people – and the odd tourist – abandoning whatever they were doing to stand by the roadside and enjoy the Tour (and scramble for freebies from the publicity caravan, though they didn't mention this). 'We had never seen such a crowd,' wrote Desgrange of one stage in 1930. 'Factories, schools, barracks, seminaries, to name but a few! Everyone had the day off. The customs officials and the gendarmes, the lumberjacks and the shepherdesses, the priests and the Capuchins, the workers and the pretty girls.'

It was a decade, too, in which the organisers commissioned songs for the race and, each year, selected an official anthem, which blared from tinny speakers attached to the vehicles that made up the *caravane publicitaire*.

It was, briefly, a golden period. But it was shattered by the outbreak of war, just a few weeks after the conclusion to the 1939 Tour. The rising tension in Europe was already having an impact in that final pre-war Tour: Germany, Spain and Italy all declined to send teams, which deprived the race of its defending champion, and one of the stars of the era, the Italian Gino Bartali. Instead, France sent no fewer than five teams, but – almost as a pre-echo of their declining fortunes post-1985 – could not supply the winner, the Belgian Sylvère Maes triumphing ahead of René Vietto, the Frenchman sometimes described as the best rider never to win the Tour.

Vietto had made his name in 1934 when, aged just 20, he won a stage in the Alps and then had to very publicly sacrifice his own chances in the Pyrenees. On stage 16 he led up the Col du Puymorens and began the descent when news reached him that his team leader, the 1931 winner Antonin Magne, had crashed and broken his front wheel. Vietto stopped, rode back up the hill, and gave Magne his wheel. Then he sat on the wall by the road, his bike propped up alongside him, waiting for a service vehicle with a spare wheel. A photographer captured the image of the forlorn Vietto, his tearful eyes cast down the road (page 47). It was a picture that instantly captured the hearts of the French people, and it endures to this day as an image of the self-sacrifice of the team rider, or domestique. It is also an image that underlines the influential role that photography can play in the Tour narrative, and in creating its myths and legends.

For instance, it is hardly known – because there didn't happen to be a photographer present – that the same thing happened the next day on another Pyrenean climb, the Portet d'Aspet, only this time Magne took Vietto's bike. Vietto still managed to finish fifth in Paris, while Magne won his second Tour (having also won in 1931). But Vietto was apparently angry over what had happened; and he grew increasingly bitter over the years. He wore the yellow jersey for 29 stages in total, but second place in 1939 was as close as he ever got to winning overall.

When war broke out a few weeks after that Tour, it seemed that the race would once again enter a hiatus. But Jacques Goddet, whose father, Victor, had been the L'Auto accountant involved in the initial discussions to establish a Tour de France, had started taking over the reins from Desgrange in 1936 (Desgrange's health was failing and he died in August 1940). Goddet had other ideas. He initially planned to hold the race with teams representing military units. Even after Germany invaded France, he proposed a week long Tour, though the Vichy regime, now governing France and collaborating with the Nazis, refused to allow it.

The British magazine Picture Post later summed up the reaction of the allies to France's determination that 'the Tour must go on!': 'The organisers got official French approval to carry on with the race, even though stretches ran right through the front – but static – lines. Only the bewildered refusal of the British, who could hardly envisage stopping a war for a bike race through their section of the front, brought the plan to naught.'

Goddet was keen to resurrect the Tour as a politically neutral event during the war years, though he dropped the idea when he realised that would be impossible without at least cooperating with the Vichy regime. Yet, as war waged, Vichy's attitude towards the Tour seemed to change, and in 1942 they ran their own version, the six-stage Circuit de France, featuring riders who used ration coupons for food, slept in dormitories and were under orders not to discard bottles or food along the route. Goddet refused to have any part in it, and, hardly surprisingly, the Circuit de France didn't capture the public imagination; it was never held again.

After the war L'Auto was forced to close, as were all the newspapers that had continued to publish during the war. In its place L'Equipe was established, appearing for the first time on 28 February 1946. Goddet naturally suggested the new paper as the logical organiser of a revived Tour de France. But it was up to the new French government to decide. There was talk of it being nationalised, but it was eventually awarded to a consortium representing the Parc des Princes, which included L'Equipe and another paper, Le Parisien libéré. But it was L'Equipe, and Goddet, who emerged as the driving force.

'The Tour reopens the era of joie de vivre,' said Goddet on the eve of the first post-war race in 1947. 'It spontaneously establishes an entirely free community, it convenes a good natured society that makes no distinctions of class or political affiliation. The giants of the road are magicians who bring a happy truce.'

To underline the Tour's perceived role in helping France to rebuild – its spirit, and its fractured infrastructure – the penultimate stage finished in the heavily bombed Normandy city of Caen. Only 25 per cent of the city remained standing, but the citizens welcomed the finish, then waved the riders off the next day for the final stage to Paris. Among the riders was René Vietto, who held the yellow jersey for 15 days, but, once again, didn't win.

Rather, an extraordinary thing happened on the road from Caen to Paris, when the third-placed rider, Jean Robic, riding not for France, but for the regional West team, attacked halfway through the 257km stage, on a hill on the outskirts of Rouen.

Robic, who had started the stage placed third overall, was easily identifiable (or perhaps not) by his leather crash helmet (he always wore one after finishing the 1944 Paris-Roubaix classic with a broken skull) and his diminutive stature. He was five-foot-two and known disparagingly as the Hobgoblin of the Brittany Moor. But he made up for his lack of height with a huge chip on his shoulder: Robic was notoriously grumpy and bad-tempered.

With Robic in his great escape was another Frenchman, Edouard Fachleitner. Pierre Brambilla, in the yellow jersey, tried to follow the move, but fell back into the peloton, which hesitated before starting to chase. In these uncertain times, they weren't sure they should be chasing two Frenchmen, thereby helping a Franco-Italian (though Brambilla would become a French citizen two years later).

As they raced towards Paris, Robic offered Fachleitner 100,000 francs to help him stay away; another reward was that Fachleitner himself would move up to second overall. And so it proved. Robic thus became the first – and still the only – rider to claim his very first yellow jersey on the final day, and therefore not wear it on any stage. In doing so, the Hobgoblin added an ironic postscript to Jacques Goddet's rousing pre-Tour speech about the 'giants of the road'.

As for Brambilla, so disgusted was he that he buried his bike in his garden.

Round the houses ▶

The peloton races through a town on the road between Caen and Dinan on stage two of the 1930 Tour.

◀ **Aubisque ordeal**

Alphonse Schepers of Belgium climbing the Col d'Aubisque during the 1931 race.

Touriste-routier ▶
Louis Peglion had earned notoriety by winning a stage in 1930 while riding as a touriste-routier rather than as a member of the national team. Here he is in 1931, a Tour in which he finished 7th overall. Riders in the *touriste-routier* category rode as individuals and usually had to organise their own food and accommodation.

A wonderful action shot, showing Frenchman
Georges Speicher leading Italian Learco Guerra
into the Parc des Princes at the conclusion to
the 1933 Tour. Speicher was the overall winner,
with Guerra second, just 4 minutes down.

Out of the darkness ▶
Italy's Edoardo Molinar emerges from the tunnel at
the summit of the Col du Galibier in 1934.

◀ **Blood from a stone**
'The Monk,' Antonin Magne, reputedly the
most difficult rider to interview, here being
interviewed after his win in 1934.

Every vantage point ▶
The 1936 Tour passes through Verdun.

The bunch passing military troops close to Amiens on stage two of
the 1936 Tour. It was a Tour that its founding father, Henri Desgrange,
attended against his doctor's wishes, after a prostate operation. He
asked for his car to be packed with cushions but admitted defeat after
this stage, which finished in Charleville. He handed over to his assistant,
Jacques Goddet, who would remain at the helm for 50 years.

Cobbled crossing

The Tour crossing Vannes, in the cycling heartland of Brittany, towards the
end of the 1937 race. It was Jacques Goddet's first Tour as director, with
Henri Desgrange retiring with ill health after 33 years at the helm. Goddet
immediately overturned one of Henri Desgrange's rules, banning gears.

Evasive action

A six-man group takes to the footpath to avoid the pavé that characterised
Paris-Roubaix, or the 'Hell of the North', the big one-day Classic held each spring.
Such cobbles are an infrequent feature of the Tour, but they featured in 1937 on
stage 2, from Lille to Charleville.

▲ **Beat the train**

Level crossings are another hazard of the Tour. If they are closed, the riders have to stop. We must assume in this picture, from 1937, that Roger Lapébie and others are crossing the rail tracks once the train has passed, rather than as it is approaching.

Family reunion ▲

Roger Lapébie, the overall winner, greets his family in the Parc des Princes at the
end of the '37 Tour.

The giants of the road, 1930–47 **59**

High crowds

Post-war optimism 1: vast crowds cheer Jean Robic, known as the 'Hobgoblin of the Brittany Moor', across the summit of the Col d'Aspin in 1947. The diminutive Robic remains the only rider to claim his first yellow jersey on the last day, as he did on the final stage to Paris in this 1947 Tour.

Packed Parc ▲

Post-war optimism 2: awaiting the finish of the Tour in the Parc des Princes.

The giants of the road, 1930–47 **61**

▲ **Street party**
Post-war optimism 3: Spectators dance in the street as they wait for the Tour.

Rehydration ▼
Riders taking water from the roadside
during the 1947 race.

The Dwarf

Maurice Archambaud being consoled after he lost the yellow jersey to Sylvère Maes in 1936. Known as 'Le Nabot' (the Dwarf), the Parisian made up for his lack of height with enormous thighs. He set the world hour record, riding 45.767km at the Vigorelli velodrome in Milan in November 1937, which stood for five years, until Fausto Coppi broke it by just 32 metres.

Police escort

The peloton, with police escort, rides through the rain and through a corridor of spectators in 1936. The crowds were bigger than usual that year, since it was the first summer of France's statutory workers' holiday.

Flowers for a champion ▲

Snaking ▶

British photographer Bert Hardy captured the riders snaking up the switchbacks of the Col du Tourmalet, the highest pass in the Pyrenees during the 1951 Tour.

The greatest show on earth, 1948–52

'The greatest show on earth' they called the Tour de France in *Picture Post*, the UK's leading photographic magazine of the 1940s and 1950s, which at its peak sold close to two million copies. The 18 August 1951 edition of the weekly devoted six pages to the Tour, having sent their star photographer, Bert Hardy, to capture an event that captivated much of Europe, but remained a mystery to most in Great Britain.

Some of Hardy's pictures are featured in this chapter, including the main one, showing the riders snaking up a pass identified in the magazine as 'Le Tourniquet'. More likely, it was the Col du Tourmalet, but what is most striking about Hardy's photographs is his focus on the fans. While most lenses were directed at the riders, Hardy seemed more interested in the people who watched: the public standing for hours by the roadside; the chefs and shopkeepers who rushed from their kitchens and shops to see the Tour pass; the girls overcome at the prospect of seeing the likes of Géminiani, Bobet, Koblet, Bartali and Coppi, who had the status of Hollywood stars; and the autograph hunters peering through the windows of the riders' hotels.

Along the route, according to the accompanying article, these fans would stand 'fifty deep [to form] a steady and almost unbroken line … Farm workers down tools; train drivers on lines running alongside the road stage "go slow" … so as to keep the riders in view as long as possible – with every passenger in the train leaning out of a window.'

The Tour was exotic, glamorous, and it transfixed the country: 'In 38 years, it has become not merely France's, but possibly the world's, most sensational sporting event … [and] the month-long focus of what almost amounts to national hysteria … No other sporting spectacle in the world draws so many spectators, causes so many arguments, or involves so much money.'

The naked commercialism of the Tour de France was noted. While many other sports clung to their amateur roots, the Tour was different – it was set up as an advertising vehicle for a newspaper; the riders relied on sponsors; and the publicity caravan preceding the race grew ever larger each year.

Picture Post went so far as to describe the Tour as 'a more-than-usually frenzied advertising onslaught.' Behind the riders, the convoy by now numbered some 300 vehicles: 'officials, mechanics, spare parts, press, radio, film, television.' And two hours in front of them, there was the publicity caravan: 'a seemingly endless stream of publicity lorries, fantastically adorned (one, this year, had a 40-foot replica of a fully rigged ship mounted on a six-ton chassis). They advertise, through loud speakers which squawk as only a French loudspeaker can, the merits of such varied things as lingerie, liquor, soap powders, and knitting wool.'

The article continued: 'Does this make it sound like a circus? Maybe in some respects it is. But, for the riders, it is still the longest and toughest bike race in the world, and only a superman can win.'

A small detail recorded in the magazine's report is the fact that Hugo Koblet, 'of Switzerland, 26 years old, son of a Zurich pastrycook, was the winner.' With his victory he was assured of £20,000, though 'before Koblet could even put foot to the ground, his manager had signed future contracts for him to ride at 35 track meetings, all over Europe, at £150 per appearance.'

There was a significant first that the magazine missed: the ascent of Mont Ventoux, the enormous 'bald mountain' that dominates the Provence region. Lucien Lazaridès, who would eventually finish third behind Koblet, was first to the summit, though the stage didn't end there, plummeting back down to finish in Avignon.

The post-Second World War Tours witnessed the emergence of a golden generation of riders. Apart from the handsome, stylish Koblet (known as *Le pédaleur de charme*), there was the ageing Gino Bartali, the Italian rider who, in 1948, won his second Tour, ten years after his first. How many more would he have won had the war not meant seven years without a race? There was also the man who became his bitter rival, Fausto Coppi, the winner in 1949 and again in '52. Coppi had also won the Giro in 1940, and so the same question applied to him: how many Tours and Giri might he have won had it not been for the war? (Coppi managed five Giri, in any case.)

In the 1951 Tour Coppi suffered food poisoning on one stage and lost 33 minutes, yet he still managed to finish 10th, 46 minutes behind Koblet. But the '51 Tour saw the best of the popular and handsome Koblet. He was said to always carry a comb and a bottle of eau de cologne in the pocket of his racing jersey. He would comb his hair on the approach to the finish, then use the eau de cologne to freshen up for the photographers' post-race pictures. In Agen, where he won the second of his five stages of the 1951 Tour, 'followers were astonished to see him sit up, blow kisses to girls and take out of his pocket a sponge soaked in water. He was barely across the line when he rinsed his face in Perrier, combed his hair, then started his stopwatch.' This was according to Philippe Brunel, writing in *L'Equipe* some fifty years later; *L'Equipe* was the newspaper that had risen from the ashes of *L'Auto*, which had been forced to close after the war. The Tour de France was put out to tender and *L'Equipe* won the right to be recognised as organiser (along, at least initially, with *Le Parisien*). Another case of *plus ça change, plus c'est la même chose*.

After the 1951 Tour, Koblet was never the same rider. And, like a staggeringly high proportion of the stars of the Tour, his life had a tragic end. Thirteen years later, amid financial and personal turmoil, with a pending divorce from his model wife, he died, aged 39, after crashing his white Alfa Romeo into a tree. It was rumoured to be suicide. He had been seen driving at speed shortly before the accident, then passing the tree twice, before ploughing headlong into it.

It was Coppi who would outshine Koblet and most other riders, not only of his era, but for all time, with his name and image still resonating throughout the cycling world. Coppi and Bartali were both superstars, but very different, Bartali a conservative and devout Catholic, while Coppi scandalised Italy by having an extra-marital affair with the so-called 'Lady in White' (Giulia Locatelli). It prompted an intervention from Pope Pius XII, who urged him to return to his wife.

Bartali, with his flat nose and bruiser's face, looked like a boxer, while the beak-nosed Coppi, with his dark shades and slicked back hair, resembled a movie star. He was the very image of perfection on the bike, his long, tanned limbs turning the pedals with velvet smoothness. It isn't difficult to imagine Coppi excelling in any era. Perhaps because he never grew old (he died of malaria in 1960, when he was 40), there is a timeless quality to these images of Coppi.

He was modern in other ways, too, being one of the first riders to have a personal soigneur (masseur), in his case the blind former boxer with magical hands, Biagio Cavanna. He was also candid about his use of drugs (amphetamines were in vogue after the war), famously telling reporters that he used them 'only when necessary.' And when was it necessary, he was asked? 'Almost always.'

This was another subject on which he and Bartali had different views, with Bartali so suspicious of Coppi that he would spy on him, entering his hotel room when he left, tiptoeing 'to the waste bin and the bedside table, [to] go through the bottles, flasks, phials, tubes, cartons, boxes, suppositories – I swept up everything. I became so expert in interpreting all these pharmaceuticals that I could predict how Fausto would behave during the course of the stage. I would work out, according to the traces of the product I found, how and when he would attack me.'

Both Bartali and Coppi were revered in Italy – Coppi as Il Campionissimo (champion of champions), Bartali as Il Pio (the pious) – and their influence stretched beyond cycling and sport as the country rebuilt after the war. Indeed, Bartali was credited with helping to prevent a political crisis in Italy during the 1948 Tour. He trailed Louison Bobet by 20 minutes when the country's prime minister, Alcide De Gasperi, is said to have urged Bartali to do something spectacular in France. Bartali then won three stages in a row and claimed overall victory in Paris by 14 minutes over Ferdi Kübler, who would win two years later. 'To say that civil war was averted by a Tour de France victory is surely excessive,' said Giulio Andreotti, the country's future prime minister. 'But it is undeniable that on that 14th of July of 1948 … Bartali contributed to ease the tensions.'

It was Coppi who won the Tour a year later, and then again in 1952, when, 42 years after Octave Lapize was the winner of the first Tour to include the high mountains, the race featured its first summit finish. Alpe d'Huez was the mountain, and the myth of that iconic place began with – and perhaps owed rather a lot to – Coppi.

It was also during this Tour that the relationship between Coppi and Bartali

seemed to warm, thanks to the infamous 'shared bottle'. As they climbed the Col d'Izoard, a photographer was on hand to capture the moment when the two appeared to share a bottle of water. Then, however, they fell out again over who had offered it first. The photograph is inconclusive: it merely shows both with their hands on it. 'I gave it to him,' said Bartali. 'He never gave me anything.'

Italians on top
Gino Bartali leads his arch rival – and that year's Tour winner – Fausto Coppi high in the mountains during the 1949 race.

Velvet smoothness

The rider known as Il Campionissimo (champion of champions), Fausto Coppi, in full flight during the 1949 Tour, the first of his two victories. Coppi was arguably the first 'modern' cyclist, and, as far as some are concerned, the ultimate stylist. He and his great rival, Gino Bartali, scored an Italian one-two in this Tour, with 'Il Pio' (the pious), second.

Hobgoblin of the Brittany moor
The 'Hobgoblin', Jean Robic rides through the crowds at the summit of the Col d'Aubisque in the Pyrenees during the 1949 Tour.

Il Campionissimo

The men at the roadside seem transfixed by the sight of Fausto Coppi racing through their town during the 1949 race. Iconic is an over- and usually inappropriately used word, but Coppi might be as close as the sport of cycling has to an icon. One explanation is that he died close to his peak, just eleven years after this picture was taken. Aged 40, he contracted malaria in Burkina Faso, though there were claims, as recently as 2002, that he was poisoned. The Coppi myth also owes something to his scandalous affair with the 'Woman in White' and the intrigue surrounding his soigneur, Biagio Cavanna, a blind former boxer and a mystical figure.

▲ **Cooling off**
A fireman hoses the peloton down during the 1950 race. Surprisingly, they were
not in the baking south but in Montmédy, in the north-east of France.

Leather head ▶

Jean Robic leads the peloton. He is identifiable by his size (1.61m) and the leather crash helmet he wore after falling and breaking his skull during the 1944 Paris-Roubaix (which he still finished). No other rider wore a helmet and another of Robic's nicknames was *tête de cuir* (leather head).

◀ Orson and Il Pio

Gino Bartali meets Orson Welles, who officially started the 1950 Tour in Paris on 13 July. The plot of this Tour, which saw Bartali withdraw following allegations that he tried to sabotage Robic by causing him to crash, was worthy of The Third Man, the film noir Welles had starred in the previous year. During stage 11, Bartali was in a break with Robic in the Pyrenees when he crashed, bringing down Robic. Bartali got back up and won the stage, but French fans were out in force and they blamed Bartali, punching and kicking him and, in one instance, threatening him with a knife. That night, Bartali withdrew from the Tour, ordering all the Italian riders to follow him.

Feeling the pressure

Maurice Blomme pumps up his tyres in Niot before the start of stage 9 of the 1950 race. Three days later, in Perpignan, Blomme was the stage winner, though he almost wasn't. He had sprinted for the finish line, then stopped. But he'd sprinted for the wrong line. An official put him back on his bike for the final few metres.

Finish in sight ▲

The peloton swings into a packed Parc des Princes for the traditional finish of the Tour in 1951. Hugo Koblet, second from the left, made it two Tour victories in a row for Switzerland, following Ferdi Kübler's win in 1950.

Pre-stage preparations
Team cars, packed with spare wheels, at a stage start during the 1951 Tour. The
picture also shows a soigneur, in vest and shorts, holding the musettes (food
bags) that he will hand up to the riders during the stage.

Majestic mountains ▽
One of Bert Hardy's photographs for *Picture Post* in 1951: a perfect illustration
of the majesty of the mountains, the suffering of the riders, and the diabolical
state of the roads.

Returning heroes ▲

The Frenchman Raphaël Géminiani kisses his wife in the Parc des Princes after finishing second in the 1951 Tour to the man standing beside him, the elegant Hugo Koblet known as the *pédaleur de charme*.

Le chef
Another of Bert Hardy's pictures shows
a chef abandoning his post to cheer the
'Giants of the Road'.

The caption in *Picture Post* seeks to explain this female fan's response to the rider (or riders) she is hoping to see: 'He's Clark Gable, Len Hutton, Denis Compton and Laurence Olivier rolled into one. She waits for hours for a glimpse of him, and a friend restrains her when she gets it. He's gone, perhaps for ever, but he leaves with her an undying memory of glory.'

Coppi cools down ▲

At first glance it isn't clear whether Fausto Coppi, on his way to winning the 1952 Tour, wants this shower, courtesy of a watering can. Closer study suggests his hand is clasped around the spout, directing it over his head.

Louison Bobet on the Bald Mountain, Mont Ventoux, its incredible moonscape
forming a surreal backdrop as he rides to victory on the stage and to his third
consecutive overall win in 1955.

Bobet and the bald mountain, 1953–60

The Giant of Provence, Mont Ventoux, was introduced to the Tour in 1951, and
also featured in '52, but it came of age four years later, as Louison Bobet bid to
become the first man to win the Tour three years in a row.

Bobet was ferociously talented and highly intelligent, but also sensitive (he
abandoned his first Tour in 1947 in tears, earning the nickname 'cry baby') and
as tightly wound as a spring. Even when he was winning he was anxious and
wracked by doubt and insecurity – in fact, he could be even worse when he
was winning.

His neurosis could manifest itself in strange ways. When Bobet took over the
lead in 1948 he was presented with a yellow jersey made by the Tour's new
sponsor, Sofil, using synthetic material. Bobet refused to accept it; he would only
wear a jersey made from pure wool. A replacement was made overnight.

Bobet's nerves were never worse than on 18 July 1955, on the 198km stage all
the way from the Mediterranean, Marseille, to Avignon, in the heart of Provence.
Ahead of them was that terrible obstacle: Mont Ventoux.

As they approached the climb, Bobet rode alongside his brother, Jean, also riding
for the French national team, to 'whisper that he's not feeling well, not well at all.'
But for Jean Bobet, 'knowing him as I do, that's a good sign.' A little further on,
Louison told Jean to ride 'on the rivet': flat out at the front. The reason was to tee
Bobet up for an attack, with which he hoped to distance the Luxembourg climber,
Charly Gaul, already becoming known as the 'angel of the mountains' after his
victory at Briançon on stage eight, after a tough day in the Alps.

As the road began to climb up the Ventoux, past the treeline, heading into the
white, lunar-like landscape of the upper slopes, the particular ferocity of this
mountain was highlighted by another of the French riders, Jean Malléjac, who
collapsed and lost consciousness. After Malléjac came to, and was taken to
hospital, the Tour doctor issued a warning to the other riders: go easy on the
amphetamines, which he reckoned had caused Malléjac to overdo it. It was an
incident that eerily foreshadowed the Tour's greatest tragedy, also on the slopes

of Mont Ventoux, twelve years later. Malléjac's collapse should have acted as a warning. It didn't.

What, precisely, made the Ventoux so torturous and demanding? At just below 2,000 metres, it is hardly the highest mountain. But the road climbs in a straight line, offering no break in the relentless slog; it is also steep, averaging 8.9 per cent for the final 16km. And there is little shelter above the treeline; despite the altitude, the temperature can soar into the forties; another difficulty is the mistral wind, which can wreak havoc, especially near the exposed summit.

It was as the slopes reared up, against the lunar backdrop, that Bobet attacked, and went clear. He crossed the summit alone and won in Avignon by six minutes, leaving him second overall, behind his teammate Antonin Rolland, but poised to win the Tour in the Pyrenees. That night in Avignon, though, Bobet's insecurities and anxieties were as pervasive as ever. Lying on his bed, with his shoes still on, he called for his brother, then 'mumbled, in snatches, that he was done in … He couldn't move … He was in pain, all over … He couldn't carry on … He'd lost everything … All that effort had been for nothing … The others would attack tomorrow.' What did trouble Bobet for the rest of the Tour, and forced him to stand on the pedals for an entire stage, was an open saddle sore that, over the following winter, would need surgery.

Perhaps that Ventoux stage really did drain Bobet of his powers, for he only finished one more Tour de France, in 1958. He was seventh.

According to Jean Bobet, the early 1950s saw a 'G4' emerge in the sport of cycling. The big four were Fausto Coppi, the Swiss riders Ferdi Kübler and Hugo Koblet, and his brother, Louison. The fifth dominant force in the post-war years, Gino Bartali, was too old by the mid-50s, and, between them, the G4 won every Tour between 1949-55. As Jean Bobet puts it in his wonderful memoir, *Tomorrow, We Ride*, 'they were so dominant that it was impossible to miss them.'

Bobet adds: 'They were not just winners. Beyond their performances they had style.' And they lived in style: Koblet with his model wife and fancy cars; Louison with his penchant for flying (he had his own plane). 'They plumped for fine hotels, fine restaurants and large cars. They lived like stars as befitted their rank. But that never distracted them from the requirements or the constraints of a profession that kept them on a tight leash. It was a profession which they held in too much respect for them to forget, even for an instant, its spartan discipline.'

THE ANGEL AND THE EAGLE

In 1957, with the G4 falling apart, a replacement emerged. But this wasn't a quartet: it was one rider, whose true dominance would tell in the next decade. His name was Jacques Anquetil, the winner of the Tour in 1957, when he was just 23.

Alone on the mountain
'I don't feel well, not well at all,' Louison Bobet told his brother, Jean, on the approach to Mont Ventoux. But as the road climbed up towards the barren summit he attacked and rode alone to victory.

Yet before Anquetil's talent fully blossomed, towards the end of the decade the Tour was won by a couple of riders, Charly Gaul and Federico Bahamontes, who were 'purs grimpeurs' – pure climbers. These riders – others over the years include Marco Pantani, Luis Herrera, Lucien Van Impe and Robert Millar – could thrill and exhilarate with their attacking riding in the mountains, though overall victories in the Tour have proved rare. Generally they are undone in the flat stages, where, with the light build that proves so beneficial in the mountains, they can struggle to hold their position near the front of the peloton, and to produce the same power as bigger riders in the time trials.

In the classic tradition, purs grimpeurs are small, quirky and eccentric. They can also be troubled. At the time of writing, the last pure climber to win the Tour was Marco Pantani in 1998, who, overcome by doping scandals, which left him paranoid and depressed, died of cocaine poisoning six years after his greatest success. His fellow climbing specialist José María Jiménez, of Spain, died in similar circumstances just a few months earlier. Five years before that, Frenchman Thierry Claveyrolat, the top climber of the early 1990s, committed suicide having also suffered from depression. And then there is the Scottish mountain goat, Robert Millar, the King of the Mountains in the 1984 Tour, who, since retirement, has vanished from the sport.

But the rider who established the blueprint for eccentric, enigmatic climbers was the 'Angel of the Mountains,' Charly Gaul. Gaul, from Luxembourg, won the Tour in 1958, but in retirement he, like Millar, simply disappeared.

Initially he opened a bar beside the main railway station in Luxembourg City, but six months later abandoned it, as well as his second wife, and vanished. He was eventually discovered living as a hermit deep in the Ardennes Forest. And for nearly two decades that was where he stayed, in a hut filled with Christian symbols and trinkets, without piped water or electricity.

To understand what a transformation this was, Gaul had been a flamboyant, popular figure – not so much with his fellow riders, towards whom he could be arrogant and antagonistic, but with the fans. At the height of his fame Gaul received 60 letters a day, virtually all from adoring female fans.

He was quirky and audacious. On the mountainous stage 21 of his victorious Tour, in 1958, Gaul, who was over sixteen minutes down overall, rode alongside Louison Bobet, and taunted him: 'You're ready, Monsieur Bobet? I'll attack on the Luitel climb. I'll even tell you which hairpin. You want to win the Tour? Easy. I've told you what you need to know.' (His hostility towards Bobet could be explained by an incident in the previous year's Giro d'Italia, when Bobet and his French teammates attacked Gaul after he stopped to answer a call of nature.)

On the hairpin in question Gaul was good to his word, attacking powerfully, early in the 219km stage. In freezing cold and torrential rain – conditions he relished – the Angel soared alone over the three mountains of the Chartreuse Massif to Aix-les-Bains, clawing back nearly all of his sixteen-minute deficit on the yellow jersey. The defending champion, Anquetil, finished 22 minutes down.

It was a brutal Tour: 24 stages, and not a single rest day. Bobet, in his final Tour, finished 31 minutes behind Gaul.

In total Gaul won ten stages in the Tour and was twice crowned King of the Mountains. Bobet described him as 'a murderous climber, always the same sustained rhythm, a little machine … turning his legs at a speed that would break your heart, tick tock, tick tock, tick tock, tick tock.' The French writer Antoine Blondin called him 'Mozart on two wheels.'

Yet even at the peak of his career, Gaul could wear a haunted expression. According to one writer he had, 'A sad, timid look on his face, marked with an unfathomable melancholy. He gives the impression that an evil deity has forced him into a cursed profession amidst powerful, implacable rivals.'

Such an observation puts a slightly different perspective on his disappearance – as does his place in the pantheon of eccentric climbers. Like so many, Gaul was, self-evidently, a loner. He lived alone for nearly 20 years in his hut in the forest, growing a long beard and a potbelly. Several journalists tracked him down, but he wouldn't speak. Gaul spent his days planting vegetables, his routine only changing for one month of the year: July. Then, he would connect his little portable television to his car battery in order to watch the Tour de France.

And then, abruptly, Gaul reappeared in 1983. His re-emergence seemed to be down to love: he remarried, had a daughter, and slowly integrated back into society. In 1989, when the Tour de France visited his native Luxembourg, he was there, standing by the roadside watching impassively. By the early 1990s he was following the sport that made his name in the flesh rather than on a small portable TV in the middle of the forest. A young Italian climber, who idolised the Angel of the Mountains, sought him out on a racing trip to Luxembourg. His name was Marco Pantani, and he and Gaul became friends.

Gaul attended Pantani's funeral in 2004 and – though by now suffering from Alzheimer's disease – he was said to be particularly upset at the death of the best climber of the modern era. Pantani had certainly been a key figure in Gaul falling – in the words of former Tour director Jean-Marie Leblanc – 'back in love with the sport like a fan.'

The year after Gaul's triumph in the Tour, it was won by another brilliant climber, Spain's Federico Bahamontes, known as the 'Eagle of Toledo', and easily identifiable by his upright climbing style. Bahamontes' victory – the first by a Spaniard – owed something to an alliance he formed with Gaul in the Alps, and also to the fact that his teammate in a multinational squad was Fausto Coppi, whose powers had waned, but who instilled in Bahamontes the belief he needed to become more than just a climbing specialist.

Other than in 1959, it was as a pure climber that Bahamontes was best known. He was crowned the Tour's King of the Mountains six times. And yet it is Gaul who remains, for many, the original pur grimpeur; and the only Angel of the Mountains. Gaul died in December 2005, two days before his 73rd birthday, after falling and hitting his head in his home in Itzig, Luxembourg.

Against the clock

Louison Bobet on his way to winning the time trial from Lyon to St Etienne, just two days from Paris and his first overall victory in 1953.

Bobet's first

Bobet does a lap of honour at the Parc des Princes. To celebrate the 50th anniversary of the Tour he was met in Paris by eleven former winners, including Maurice Garin, winner of the first Tour in 1903.

▲ **It's no picnic**
To this day French families set up their picnics by the roadside – *baguettes, fromage, vin* – and await the arrival of the Tour. Here is one family in 1954, though the parents seem more interested than the children.

Bobet, with his familiar haunted expression, leads an elite group on the slopes of the Col d'Izoard on the road to Briançon in 1954. Behind him are Ferdi Kübler and Jean Mallejac. Bobet won the stage en route to his second consecutive Tour victory.

Hat-trick
Bobet celebrates becoming the first man to win three consecutive Tours, from 1953 to 1955.

Keeping up with the Angel
Bobet tries to match the murderous rhythm of the great Luxembourg climber, Charly Gaul, in the 1955 Tour.

COL DE LA CAYOLLE
Alt. 2326m

Angel of the mountains ▲

Noses in the trough

Raids on bars for drinks were common – not least because the Tour organisers
limited the number of bidons they were allowed during a stage – though the
riders would hydrate whenever the opportunity arose. Here some riders drink
from a roadside trough in 1958.

Future perfect
A young Jacques Anquetil, who was just 23 when he won his first Tour in 1957. Note the immaculate hair: like Hugo Koblet, he carried a comb in his pocket.

Lining the streets
The peloton sweeps through crowd-lined streets during the 1958 route.

▲ **Angel attack**
Charly Gaul, in the wet, cold conditions in which he thrived, on the Col de Porte on his way to winning the 21st stage and the 1958 Tour. He had told Louison Bobet exactly where he would attack, but nobody could follow.

Eagle attack ▲

The other great climber of the era, Spain's Federico Bahamontes on the road to
Grenoble in 1959; Gaul won the stage but Bahamontes, a terrible descender,
claimed the yellow jersey, and in Paris became Spain's first Tour winner.

Signing ▶

René Privat from the Mercier team signs an autograph for a female fan, in 1957, when he won three stages and wore yellow for three days. Mercier, the French bicycle manufacturer, sponsored a team from 1935-69.

▼ **Broom wagon**

The 'voiture balai' is the broom wagon, the last vehicle in the convoy that follows the Tour and 'sweeps up' any rider who wishes to retire. In this picture from the mid-1950s it follows the last rider on the road as he endures a lonely battle for survival. The bikes on the roof indicate that some riders may already have abandoned, and will be sitting inside.

Three of the best ▲

A rare colour image from the 1959 Tour showing three of the best riders of the
era: Bahamontes, Gaul and Rivière.

End of the road for Rivière

The tragic Roger Rivière was favourite to win the 1960 Tour and was sitting second to Italy's Gastone Nencini with his strongest discipline, the time trial, to come. But while attempting to follow Nencini, an ace descender, off the Col de Perjuret, he hit a low wall and fell into the ravine; he would later reveal that he had taken painkillers that could have affected his judgement and contributed to the collision. It was the end of his career; he broke his spine, never recovered full use of his limbs and was thereafter confined to a wheelchair. Rivière died of throat cancer aged 40.

Shoulder to shoulder ▶

Anquetil and Poulidor do battle in one of
the Tour's epic duels on the steep slopes of
the Puy-de-Dôme in 1964.

Master Jacques and the eternal second, 1961–68

There is a ubiquitous presence at every Tour de France. He wears a yellow short-sleeved shirt, and hangs around the Village Départ.

Now in his mid-70s, he wears glasses, has white hair, a flat nose and a friendly face. His presence has spanned the Bernard Hinault years as well as the eras of Miguel Indurain and Lance Armstrong, and he will no doubt be around for as long as he is able, to hold court each morning, sign autographs and pose for pictures.

Raymond Poulidor is more popular than many – perhaps most – of the current riders. But being popular is one of the two things he is best known for. The other is for not winning the Tour.

Poupou, as he is known, never even wore the yellow jersey. He was a dashing, dark-haired, olive-skinned rider from a humble farming family in central France, who became known as the 'eternal second'. He finished runner-up at the Tour three times, and third on another five occasions. He started 14, finished 12 and won seven stages, but, astonishingly, yellow always eluded him. At least these days, in his capacity as a guest of Crédit Lyonnais bank, sponsors of the maillot jaune, he gets to wear a yellow shirt. A pity it has buttons and a collar.

Poulidor was unlucky to come up against Jacques Anquetil and, later, Eddy Merckx. Then again, his popularity, especially among the French, possibly owed rather a lot to the fact that he didn't win, and perhaps also that he wasn't Anquetil. Their rivalry divided France in the same way that the Coppi–Bartali rivalry had split Italy, if not to a greater extent. Maître Jacques represented the modern 'win-at-all-costs mentality', whereas Poupou was a man of the people, who could identify with his humble origins and his suffering.

Yet there was a negative aspect to Poulidor's popularity, which has persisted to this day. His name has come to be so associated with the plucky loser that it

has become representative of all losers, and a self-fulfilling prophecy; a 'Poulidor complex' can describe anyone from politicians to sportsmen. But the man himself is pragmatic, perhaps even a little proud: 'My name has passed into the everyday language. It's my greatest victory.' (Though not, despite his 'eternal second' nickname, his only victory. He may not have claimed the sport's ultimate prize, but he did win seven stages and numerous other big races including Paris–Nice.)

Anquetil's lack of popularity, meanwhile, owed something to his aloof personality, but also to the way he rode. The blonde-haired, blue-eyed, sharp-cheekboned rider from Normandy was metronomic and calculating. He wasn't a Fausto Coppi, a Charly Gaul or a Federico Bahomontes – riders capable of dynamiting the race in the mountains with their explosive attacks. Anquetil did not have their, or Poulidor's, climbing gifts, or the panache that went with it. And so he relied on something else – his ability against the watch. He was arguably the first time trial specialist, and certainly the first to use this ability as the foundation for his Tour victories, which, by 1964, numbered a record five. After his first success in 1957, he won four in a row from 1961.

It is an image from the 1964 Tour that encapsulates the rivalry between Anquetil and Poulidor. In many ways it also encapsulates the qualities of a Tour winner: the ability to endure, to suffer. Anquetil was, according to some commentators, 'the man who can't be dropped, but who can drop no one.' It had taken him until the previous year, 1963, to win his first mountain stage, after riding hard up the Col du Tourmalet and then winning a sprint in Bagnerres de Bigore.

The 1964 Tour was his toughest, and not merely because of his battle with Poulidor on the road. There was stress in the build-up, too, with a 'seer', Jacques Belline, predicting in *France Soir* that Anquetil would die in a crash on the 14th stage. Aloof and cool he might have been, but this naturally upset Anquetil. According to his manager Raphaël Géminiani – one of the top riders of the 1950s – he reacted to the article 'as if he'd been smacked in the face.'

The day before the fateful 14th stage was a day off in Andorra, and Anquetil broke with the Tour rider's usual rest day routine of training. Instead, he and Géminiani enjoyed a lavish lamb barbecue washed down with wine. This was not untypical Anquetil behaviour. As well as taking pride in his appearance (including carrying a comb in his pocket, *à la* Hugo Koblet), he was quite the *bon vivant*, telling his friend André Darrigade, on the eve of his first Tour, that he would take a suit, so that he could go out in the evenings. He also smoked, 'but only on rest days during the Tour.'

The day after the rest day – the day of Anquetil's predicted demise – took the riders to Toulouse, with the climb of the Col d'Envalira tackled early. It was shrouded in fog, which thickened on the descent, making conditions extremely dangerous. But Anquetil's problems started before the descent, when Poulidor, Julio Jiménez and Federico Bahamontes attacked, building a lead of over five minutes by the summit. The Tour looked to be over for Anquetil, until Géminiani urged him to chase: 'For God's sake if you're going to die, you might as well die at the front.'

As the front group tackled the corners gingerly in the fog, Anquetil plummeted like a stone and caught them. Three days later he won his speciality, the time trial, to take the yellow jersey, but his lead over Poulidor was too slender for comfort: just 56 seconds.

Their battle came down to the vicious little climb of an extinct volcano in the Massif Central, the Puy de Dôme. At 1,465m, the mountain juts above the town of Clermont-Ferrand in the heart of the Auvergne, in the dead centre of France. It isn't the longest, but it is one of the hardest, since the road steepens as it rises.

When the Spanish climbers Jiménez and Bahamontes danced away, Anquetil let them go. He was three-and-a-half minutes ahead of the Eagle of Toledo, and so the only man he had to watch, and mark, was Poulidor. Which is precisely what he did.

The scene that then played out on the Puy de Dôme remains one of the strangest the Tour has ever witnessed. While traditionally riders follow each other, gaining shelter as the man in front breaks the wind, here Anquetil tried a novel tactic. He rode alongside Poulidor. 'All I cared was that I was directly next to Raymond,' he said afterwards. 'I needed to make him think I was as strong as he, to bluff him into not trying harder.'

The series of pictures on p.101 captures their *mano-a-mano* battle in all its epic, heroic, strange glory. They appear so grimly focused on negotiating the mountain that they do not notice that they are shoulder-to-shoulder, elbow-to-elbow. Even when physical contact is made, they don't alter their line, or check their effort; their eyes remain glued to the road, their faces registering only the effort of tackling this tough, steep climb. It is as though they are simultaneously supremely aware of, and totally oblivious to, the other. (Poulidor said afterwards that no contact was made, though the photographs prove otherwise.)

'I looked up at the *flamme rouge* [the red kite, signifying a kilometre to go] flapping in the breeze and thought, I'll make it now,' said Anquetil later. But allowing his focus to drift from his shoulder-to-shoulder battle with Poulidor proved costly. 'In that moment my attention lapsed. Poulidor had a length on me, a length I couldn't make up. I nearly collapsed.'

As Poulidor rode away in the final kilometre, and Anquetil tried to peg him back, the gap opened to 42 seconds. 'How much?' Anquetil asked Géminiani after crossing the line, and collapsing on his bike.

'You still have 14 seconds,' he was told.

'That's 13 more than I need,' Anquetil replied.

Later, he admitted: 'If Poulidor had taken the jersey I'd have gone home.' He went on to win his fifth, and final, Tour in Paris. 'My pride comes from beating a great champion in the hardest Tour I've known,' he said. For his part, Poulidor, said: 'All he was interested in was winning, by one second, two seconds – it didn't matter. He had a watch in his head.'

The argument can be made that Anquetil was misunderstood. He foreshadowed Miguel Indurain, another rider whose Tour victories were established on the bedrock of his supreme time trialling ability. It was hardly their fault that their strongest discipline is the least exciting to watch, but it meant that they were admired rather than loved.

But sometimes even admiration eluded Anquetil. In 1961, when he was perhaps at the height of his powers, yet also at his most calculating, his strength and defensive riding stifled the race. His rivals knew they could not beat him, and so didn't try, prompting Jacques Goddet, the Tour director, to describe them in L'Equipe as 'dwarves of the road' (a deliberate contrast with his predecessor Henri Desgrange's paean to the 'giants of the road' in the 1930s). 'Yes, fearful dwarves, either impotent, as Gaul has become, or resigned to their mediocrity, content simply with a good placing,' wrote Goddet, his pen dripping acid. 'Little men who have managed to save themselves, to avoid inflicting pain – cowards who above all are scared of suffering.'

Yet Anquetil, a little like Indurain, was perhaps a victim of his own class. He looked as though he was born on a bike; he was so smooth that he didn't betray any suffering. Which was a problem, since images of suffering – as Desgrange and Goddet made clear in their columns – were precisely what people wanted from the Tour de France.

It went too far three years after Anquetil and Poulidor's epic tussle. Then, the willingness of one rider to suffer beyond his natural limits had a fatal outcome. It had been anticipated in 1955 by Jean Malléjac's collapse on the barren slopes of Mont Ventoux, but Tom Simpson's battle with his bike, and himself, towards the summit of the Bald Mountain on stage 13, on July 13, of the 1967 Tour, ended in terrible tragedy.

It was a day in which the temperature soared into the 40s, prompting the Tour doctor, Pierre Dumas – who had also attended to Malléjac, and issued his warning then about the use of amphetamines – to remark: 'If the riders take something today we'll have a death on our hands.'

Simpson, who had become the first British rider to wear the yellow jersey in 1962, began the 1967 race with a towering sense of ambition. He was a brilliant rider who had won most of the major one-day events, but he was limited over the three weeks of the Tour. He reckoned that stage 13 was make-or-break, but,

as the slopes of the Ventoux wound up to its moonscape summit, he couldn't stay with the leaders, and fell back to a chase group, which he repeatedly attempted to leave. It was no use; he couldn't get away. Simpson weaved from one side to the other, trying to ease the gradient, but eventually fell to the road. He got up and insisted on carrying on, telling his mechanic, Harry Hall, to tighten his toe-straps, even as Hall tried to persuade him to stop.

When, close to the top, he collapsed again, his hands still gripping the bars, he still wanted to carry on. 'Go on, go on!' he told Hall, which was falsely reported as 'Put me back on my bike!' in the Sun newspaper, and passed into legend. They were his last words. When Dumas arrived, he gave Simpson mouth-to-mouth resuscitation, massaged his chest and fitted him with an oxygen mask. But he was no longer breathing. He was taken by a police helicopter to hospital in Avignon but was pronounced dead soon after his arrival, at 5.30pm.

Amphetamines were found in his pocket, and Dumas seemed determined to finally alert the riders to the dangers of the drugs they were using. He refused to sign a burial certificate until an autopsy was arranged. It revealed that Simpson died of a heart attack, and that he had drugs in his system. He had pushed his body too far, with the heat, the drugs, the alcohol (he drank brandy early in the stage – riders believed, falsely, that alcohol could enhance performance), and the effort all combining to kill him.

The following year's Tour was billed the Tour de la Santé, the Tour of good health, and symbolically started in Vittel, famous for its natural mineral water. Stages were shorter, there were daily drugs tests, but – as illustrated by the fact that there would be other attempts to reboot the Tour – the doping did not stop, despite Simpson's death.

Something else didn't change. Poulidor still could not win the Tour. There was a slick transition from one era to the next with Anquetil retiring in 1969, the year of Eddy Merckx's first Tour victory. But there is a poignant footnote to the rivalry that divided France in the 1960s. It comes from 1987, as Anquetil lay in hospital in Rouen, dying of stomach cancer at the age of just 53. When Poulidor visited his old foe he spoke to him, as Poulidor recalled: 'He said to me that the cancer was so agonisingly painful that it was like racing up the Puy de Dôme all day, every hour of the day. He then said, I will never forget it, "My friend, you will come second to me once again."'

◀ **Full flight**

Jacques Anquetil leads the peloton around the Parc des Princes on the final stage of the 1961 Tour, his second victory. He was doing a sterling team job here, too, leading out his French teammate Robert Cazala for the stage win.

Encore Anquetil

The podium in 1961: Guido Carlesi, Anquetil and Charly Gaul, who lost second place on the final day, by two seconds. Anquetil was dominant, taking yellow on stage 2 and wearing it all the way to Paris. ▶

Blood sport ▲

The courage of the crash victim: Joseph
Thomin battles to rejoin the peloton after a
nasty crash in 1962.

▲ **Poulidor complex**

Raymond Poulidor, the 'eternal second', leads the bunch in the mountains in 1962. It was the first Tour since 1929 contested by 'trade' (professional) teams rather than nations.

Major Tom ▶
It has taken 59 years for a British cyclist to
wear the yellow jersey: Tom Simpson wore it
for a day after stage 12 in 1962.

Master Jacques
Cheekbones like razor blades, Maître Jacques
(Anquetil) cuts an impressive figure when in
full flight. Here he is on stage 19 in the Alps in
1962, on his way to Tour number 3.

Into thin air
Poulidor and Federico Bahamontes lead the
bunch through the mountains during the
1963 race.

Roadside distraction ▼
Some fans abandon the beach to wave
the Tour past in 1964. The race skirted the
Mediterranean en route to the Pyrenees,
with Jacques Anquetil eventually winning
for a fifth time.

▲ **Ready to go**
Jacques Goddet's new co-director of the Tour, Félix Lévitan, stands in his *L'Equipe* emblazoned car, ready to wave the bunch off from Monaco for stage 10a of the 1964 Tour.

Rivals united

Jacques Anquetil and Raymond Poulidor in the Parc des Princes at the end
of the 1964 race. It was Anquetil's fifth victory, a record. Poulidor, the eternal
second, was … second. In fact, it was his first time as runner-up; he would finish
second twice more, and third on five occasions.

Tragic Tom
Simpson in action on the day of his death, 13 July 1967. His collapse was attributed to a combination of extreme heat, alcohol and amphetamines. Drugs were found in the rear pocket of his jersey; on drugs, he reportedly said: 'If it takes ten to kill you, I'll take nine.'

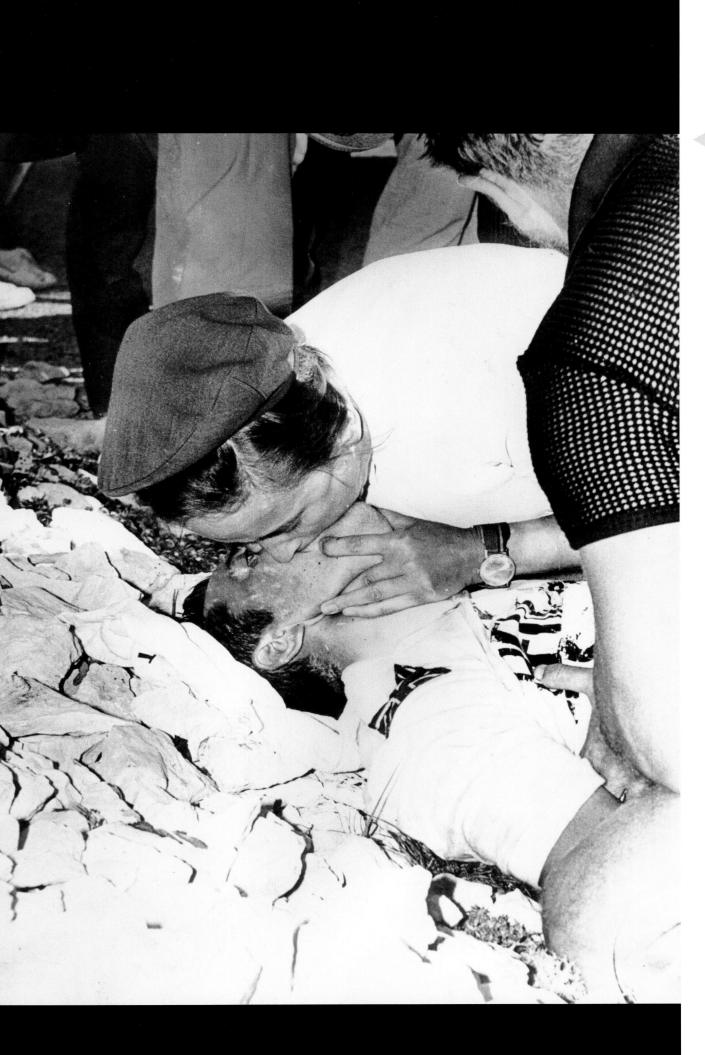

▶ **Death on the mountain**
Tom Simpson, after collapsing near the summit of Mont Ventoux on stage 13 of the 1967 Tour, is given the kiss of life. It is too late: aged 29, he is declared dead in hospital at Avignon at 5pm.

Eternal second on the attack

Raymond Poulidor leads the bunch in the Pyrenees, on stage 11 of the 1968
Tour. Four days later he was hit by a car and had to withdraw from the race.

Tour busker ▶
There is often some horseplay on the final, processional stage into Paris. It isn't clear whether this rider played the instrument for his colleagues, though his upstretched arm suggests he may be singing …

▼ The plateau
The peloton, stretched to breaking point, snakes through this mountain pass, on a plateau between snow-capped peaks.

⚠ Puffing

Gastone Nencini, the 1960 winner and a chain smoker, enjoys a cigarette.
The Tour de France mirrored wider society in the 1950s and '60s: smoking
was not only commonplace, it was cool. Some continued into the 1980s.
The Scottish rider Robert Millar asked not to share a room with his Peugeot
teammate Roger Legeay in the early 1980s because of Legeay's smoking habit.

Gorge crossing
France is famous for its spectacular works of engineering and here the peloton meanders across an extraordinary viaduct that appears to be carved out of the mountains.

▲

Finest Champagne
The 1963 peloton passes a giant bottle of
Besserat de Bellefon, from Épernay in the
heart of the Champagne region.

Domestique duties

A domestique on drinks duties fills his
pockets with liquid refreshments to carry
up to his leader. Normally he would collect
'bidons' (water bottles) from the team car,
but in these days they would take what they
could, often raiding bars or shops to collect
cold drinks.

Kamikaze cannibal ▶

Eddy Merckx on his epic, 130km solo escape in the Pyrenees, during his first
Tour in 1969. He won in Mourenx by almost eight minutes. 'Merckxissimo!'
declared Jacques Goddet in the following day's *L'Equipe*.

The cannibal, 1969–77

It started on 15 July 1969, with stage 17 of the Tour, through the Pyrenees, from
Luchon to Mourenx.

Eddy Merckx, not yet known by the nickname that would come to define
him, began the day in the yellow jersey, with an eight-minute lead on his
nearest rivals, Roger Pingeon, the ubiquitous Raymond Poulidor, and the classy
Italian, Felice Gimondi. There were five days to Paris and only one more stage
remaining with a serious climb, the Puy de Dôme. The Tour was as good as over.

But the concept of the race being over before it was over was alien to the
24-year-old Merckx, riding his first Tour. The 214km stage crossed five monstrous
passes: the Peyresourde, the Aspin, the majestic Tourmalet, the Soulor and
the Aubisque. The stage got off to an aggressive start, but the top riders were
together as they climbed to the 2,115-metre summit of the Tourmalet.

Towards the top, a teammate of Merckx, Martin Van Den Bossche, who had
attacked earlier, had a small lead, but then, abruptly, none other than Merckx
himself exploded out of the pack. He hunted down Van Den Bossche, passing
him before the line – he would be crowned King of the Mountains in his debut
Tour, as well as winning the yellow and green jerseys – then plummeting down
the other side.

In the valley his Faema team car pulled alongside and he was told to wait for
the group to catch him. There were 130km remaining: it was madness to remain
out in front alone. Merckx nodded. Then his team car punctured. He was alone.
He had a sizeable gap. He felt strong. 'At that point,' he said later, 'for the first
time, I thought it might be worth attempting an exploit in the context of such a
beautiful mountain stage. I pressed on and dug deeper than ever before.'

By the start of the Col d'Aubisque, Merckx had six minutes' lead on his pursuers.
By the summit, it had stretched to eight. Then he began to suffer from not
eating enough; he lost two minutes, but ate some food and recovered. Still
they couldn't get close; at the finish, Michele Dancelli led home the next group,
seven minutes, 56 seconds behind Merckx.

In *L'Equipe* next day Jacques Goddet coined a new term: 'Merckxissimo.' But it was another name that stuck. 'The Cannibal', as he was called by a young French rider, Christian Raymond, immediately captured the imagination, describing perfectly Merckx's insatiable appetite for winning. It was a hunger encapsulated by Merckx's overhauling of his teammate, Van Den Bossche, on the approach to the summit of the Tourmalet, so that he could claim the King of the

Mountains points on offer at the top. 'Eddy Merckx, today a small rider expected a big gesture from you,' Van Den Bossche told him in Mourenx that evening. According to Van Den Bossche, he didn't respond. 'We never spoke about such things. Eddy himself didn't talk much.'

This tells something of the paradox of Merckx. On the bike, he was a brute: a big,

 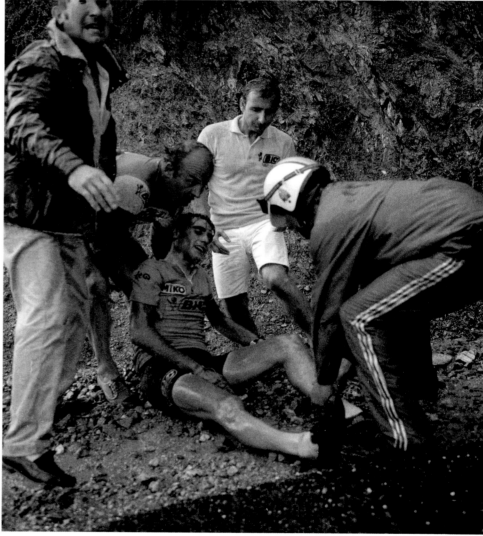

▲ **Down and out**
Luis Ocaña crashed on the descent of the Col de Menté in the 1971 Tour, then was hit by another rider as he got back to his feet. He retired while in yellow, ending his great duel with Merckx.

strong, threshing machine of a rider. Off it, he could be quiet, shy, reserved and, most surprising of all, racked by doubts and insecurities. The only way he could quell those, it seemed, was to win. Whereas other champions, most notably Jacques Anquetil, had been more calculating, Merckx wanted – or needed – to win every race he started. That wasn't possible, of course, but the Belgian achieved the highest wins-to-starts ratio of any cyclist in history, with, by the time he retired in 1978, over 500 professional victories.

There were other differences between Merckx and Anquetil. 'Anquetil appeared without warning, as silent and deadly as a dagger in the back,' writes Daniel Friebe in *Eddy Merckx: The Cannibal*. 'His pedal stroke was soft, velvety. He arrived with a murmur. He was gone with a whoosh.' Whereas, 'You heard Merckx. Felt him. Not necessarily sounds but signs, a sense. The feeling of something brewing, stirring at your back … Not the normal whirring of pedals but a thudding through the atmosphere … The rustling wrath of the "one man forest fire" that Italian rider Giancarlo Ferretti said came upon professional cycling in the late 1960s – and destroyed everything in its wake for nearly a decade.'

The names of the riders 'destroyed' by Merckx over those ten years include some who, at any other time, might have won multiple Tours. Perhaps most famously, they include Luis Ocaña, the Spaniard who won the Tour once, in 1973. It was the year Merckx was missing, having opted to ride the other two Grand Tours, of Spain and Italy, instead.

The Ocaña–Merckx rivalry was at its most intense in 1971. Ocaña drew first blood, attacking on stage 8, finishing at the top of the steep volcano, the Puy de Dôme, to steal time back on Merckx, who was in yellow. Then on stage 10, in the Alps, as Bernard Thévenet (himself a future double Tour winner) won in Grenoble, with Ocaña claiming more time, Merckx lost the yellow jersey to Joop Zoetemelk. It was the first time he had ever lost the lead of the Tour to a rider who was not a teammate.

And for Goddet it was a turning point. No more 'Merckissimo': 'Nothing will ever be the same again,' wrote the Tour director. 'If the beautiful bird has been deplumed, he will probably still be the eagle of this sport for some time. But he's no longer out of reach. He will no longer be able to dictate the outcome of races and the way they are won on his own, at the command of his omnipotence.'

Dangerous words. First, however, there was another sign that this could be Ocaña's year, on the final day in the Alps, from Grenoble to Orcières-Merlette. Thirteen kilometres into the stage, on the vicious slopes of the Côte de Laffrey, Ocaña attacked. It was reminiscent, in its audacity, of Merckx's exploit on the road to Mourenx two years earlier. Three riders went with him, including the yellow-jerseyed Zoetemelk. Merckx could not follow; and neither, eventually, could Ocaña's three companions, whom he left behind as, further back, Merckx led the chase, towing the peloton along almost single-handedly for close to 100km.

Ocaña won the stage, an astonishing eight minutes, 42 seconds ahead of Merckx. He now held the yellow jersey. Merckx had slipped to fifth, seemingly out of

contention. But Goddet and the others who had written him off had, of course, underestimated the great Belgian. He was about to surprise them all again.

The next day's stage should have been uneventful, starting with a descent and finishing, 251km later, in Marseille.

But that morning, according to *The Cannibal*, a rider from a rival team heard a strange whirring noise coming from a room in the bowels of the hotel in which the riders were staying. When he investigated he found Merckx warming up on a set of rollers. Clearly he had something in mind. And, as soon as the stage started, he put his plan into action, attacking hard with two teammates. According to one of them, they 'went off like an atomic bomb.'

For the entire stage Merckx and his nine breakaway companions raced towards Marseille between one and two minutes ahead of a peloton led by a frantic Ocaña and his Bic team. So fast was the stage that they arrived in Marseille way ahead of schedule and finished in front of sparse, unprepared crowds. Crucially, the VIPs, including the mayor, Gaston Deferre, missed the action entirely, prompting Deferre to rage: 'The Tour de France will never set foot in this city again, as long as I live.' (And it didn't. The next visit was in 1989, following Deferre's death.)

Merckx 'only' gained two minutes, 12 seconds on that stage, but the psychological blow to Ocaña was more significant. Indeed, to this day there are those who maintain that the seeds of Ocaña's downfall in the 1971 Tour were sown on the stage to Marseille. Merckx won the following day's time trial to edge closer, and then, after a rest day, they were in the Pyrenees, facing up to a 214km stage to Luchon. As they climbed the Col de Menté, Merckx had a dig, and Ocaña responded as, among the peaks of the mountains, dark clouds began to gather.

As Merckx continued to attack, and Ocaña responded – needlessly, in his teammates' view – to his every acceleration, the storm broke. It made conditions dangerous as they began the descent. And so it proved: both overshot a left hand hairpin, first Merckx, then Ocaña, who tumbled into the verge. Merckx got straight back up, but, as he was getting on his bike, Ocaña was hit by another rider – either Zoetemelk or Joaquim Agostinho; footage of the incident is inconclusive. Ocaña was hit square in the trunk; the blow floored him again. By the wet roadside he lay on the road screaming in pain. His Tour was over. He was taken by helicopter to Saint Gaudens, but there is an enduring mystery about just how serious his injuries were. Though he lost consciousness in the helicopter, the diagnosis at the hospital was that he was suffering from 'thoracic contusions and a pronounced state of shock.' He was discharged the next day. Was his destruction psychological?

Merckx, who took over the race lead in Luchon, refused to wear the yellow jersey the following day. It was a symbolic gesture of sympathy for his fallen rival, but it didn't prevent him winning his third consecutive Tour. The Cannibal – cycling's only equivalent to Muhammad Ali or Pele – would add two more, as well as every other major race on the calendar.

Threshing machine ▶
Merckx in time trial mode, on the 20th stage of the 1971 Tour to Paris. He won the stage and his third consecutive Tour.

▼ **Through and off**
Merckx, in Belgian champion's jersey, leads a breakaway on the road to Amiens during stage 5b of the 1970 race. There were split (double) stages on no fewer than five days; in one day they did 94.5km in the morning, 223km in the afternoon.

Day of reckoning ▲
Merckx, being trailed by his great rival Luis Ocaña, and the Belgian climber
Lucien van Impe, during the 1971 Tour. It was the day of Ocaña's famous crash,
which put him out of the race – and cost him arguably his best chance of
beating Merckx. Opinion on whether he would have done is still divided today.

Homing in on history ▶

In 1972 Merckx matched Jacques Anquetil's
record of four Tour victories in a row. Here he is
en route to winning the stage 5b time trial in
Bordeaux.

Merckx on the podium in Paris in 1972 presenting his green jersey to his bitter rival Cyrille Guimard, who had won four stages, worn the yellow jersey for eight stages and matched Merckx in the mountains before succumbing to a knee injury and withdrawing two days before Paris. It looks like a sporting gesture, but was instigated by the Tour organisers. Merckx and Guimard didn't like each other then, and the enmity remains to this day.

Three-way battle
Merckx battles Luis Ocaña and Raymond Poulidor on Mont Ventoux in 1972, in a picture that bears some resemblance to Poulidor's famous shoulder-to-shoulder fight with Jacques Anquetil on the Puy de Dôme eight years earlier.

Finally Ocaña gets his chance. With Merckx's sponsors
demanding that he ride the Giro d'Italia and Vuelta
a España, he didn't start in France and the Spaniard
wins his first and only Tour in 1973.

Spanish climbers rule

Ocaña and José Manuel Fuente, his fellow Spanish climber, on the Alpine climb of the Col d'Izoard in 1973. Ocaña won the stage in Les Orres.

Still second

While Ocaña seized his chance in Merckx's absence, the original 'eternal second', Raymond Poulidor, blew it. He crashed on the 13th stage and was taken away in an ambulance.

An aerial view of the peloton as it passes through Brest during the 1974 Tour.
Among the teams represented are Peugeot, Kas, Molteni and Brooklyn, sporting
some of the iconic jerseys, and small peaked caps, from what many will agree
was, certainly in terms of aesthetics, a golden era for the sport.

In memoriam

During the 1970 Tour the race director Jacques Goddet, holding a wreath, approaches the Tom Simpson Memorial close to the summit of Mont Ventoux, where the Englishman collapsed and died in 1967. In the background, Merckx rides past, on his way to winning the stage. Merckx had been Simpson's Peugeot teammate when he died, and was the only one to attend his funeral in England.

Final bow ▶
In Aix-les-Baines Merckx sprints to win stage 10 of the 1974 Tour, which would prove to be his fifth and final victory.

◀ **A new champion**
Bernard Thévenet, the man who ended the reign of Merckx in 1975, climbing Mont Ventoux in 1972, on his way to winning the 11th stage.

▲ **Impish**
The Belgian climber Lucien Van Impe, the
1976 winner, was not renowned for his
aggression, and only landed the killer blow
after his team director, the now-retired
Cyrille Guimard, threatened to run him off
the road if he didn't attack his rivals

Merckissimo

A sequence of shots from Merckx's most famous day in the saddle, during his break to Mourenx in 1969. He claimed that this, his debut Tour, saw him at his peak. A terrible crash in the velodrome at Blois at the end of the season killed his pacer; Merckx was knocked unconscious, cracked a vertebra and twisted his pelvis. He would later say he was never the same again, though he did win four more Tours.

Jacques and Eddy ▶

The two five-time winners of the Tour, Jacques Anquetil and Eddy Merckx, meet during the 1969 race. Anquetil officially retired in 1969, though he had started his last Tour in 1966, failing to finish. In retirement, he rode his bike just three times. He said he had ridden enough.

▽ **The Champs**

The Tour first finished on the Champs-Élysées in 1975, and has finished there every year since.

Bunched up

The policeman's hat gives it away: the peloton during the visit to Great Britain in 1974. Unlike more recent visits, the impetus came from the French, with Brittany's farmers keen to use new ferry links to highlight trade opportunities. It wasn't popular with the riders, though, who were kept waiting at immigration before being permitted to board the ferry back to France.

The badger, 1978–85

By 1978 the natives were restless. The riders had had enough: enough of the split-days, with their double stages, horrendous distances, early starts and late finishes; enough of being treated as expendable labour while the organisers' coffers swelled.

Split-stages, in particular, were lucrative for the organisation, since it could mean two start towns and two finish towns, with all four paying handsomely for the privilege. There had been five in 1977, and although only two followed the next year, it was, as far as some were concerned, two too many.

But in the absence of the Cannibal, Eddy Merckx, who, a broken man after battling with injuries and form, retired in March 1978, there was no rider who seemed able to articulate the riders' gripes. There was nobody with the requisite stature or authority; nobody to whom the organisers would listen; no *patron* of the peloton.

Jacques Goddet was still at the helm, as he had been since 1936, though assisted since 1962 by Félix Lévitan. The unyielding authority established by the Tour's founder, Henri Desgrange, remained intact. Though some of the riders had become stars, the vast majority had not; for them, life as a professional cyclist was no more glamorous, or better paid, than working in a factory or on a farm. They were still, to a large extent, 'workers of the pedal.'

The date and place where the balance between the organisation and the riders began to shift can be identified very precisely: to 11 July 1978, and the small town of Valence d'Agen in the Midi-Pyrénées region. It was here that a new *patron* emerged, but what is most remarkable is that he was a 23-year old Tour debutant. His name? Bernard Hinault.

Despite his youth, Hinault's first appearance at the Tour had been eagerly anticipated. Under the guidance of the now-retired Cyrille Guimard, he had been held back; even when he won Ghent–Wevelgem, Liège–Bastogne–Liège and the Dauphiné Libéré in 1977, Guimard stuck to his original plan, which meant not riding the Tour until 1978. On the eve of his debut he won the French road race

championship. And so he began his first Tour in the tricolore jersey as national champion, with some predicting that he would swap it for yellow.

Hinault's nickname, Le Blaireau (the Badger), was already starting to stick, because most agreed that it suited him. Far from being the cuddly creature of cartoons or children's stories, badgers are vicious, especially if backed into a corner. Hinault, equally defined by his Breton roots, relished the comparison with such determined, stubborn and ferocious creatures. 'They're a bit nasty,' he said in 2010, 'like me.'

But there was always more to Hinault than nastiness; he did inspire fear, but also respect. This was evident on the morning of 11 July 1978, as the riders gathered for stage 12a of the Tour. The morning stage, starting at 8am in Tarbes, was 148km; after two hours repose in Valence d'Agen, they would go again, for 96km to Toulouse, with yet another 150km bus transfer after that stage. Exacerbating the riders' unhappiness, and tiredness, they had finished late the previous evening, reaching their hotels in Tarbes at 11pm. Then they ate dinner, and had their massages, before setting alarms for 5am. Hinault didn't get to bed until 1am.

When they rose the next morning, there were stirrings of revolt. 'I remember we had started talking a little about a possible protest,' Lucien Van Impe, the great Belgian climber, would later say. 'It was yes, no, yes, no [to a strike]. Then Bernard said: "We are going on strike." And all the others agreed.'

'We were all panicking a little [about the ramifications of a strike],' said Jean-René Bernadeau, another rider. 'But Hinault said: "Do not move before I do."'

Riding near the head of the peloton, Hinault dictated the pace, which was funereal. They arrived in Valence d'Agen over an hour-and-a-half later than expected. The crowd was restless, especially when the riders did finally appear, ambling along at walking pace, and then, within sight of the finish line, stopping altogether. Hinault stood at the head of the pack, apparently oblivious to the boos and catcalls, his arms behind his back, his head tilted back, adopting a Napoleonic pose that would come to define the Badger. There was absolutely no question about who was in charge.

When Hinault gave the signal, the riders followed him, pushing their bikes towards the line. Still the crowd jeered. Still Hinault was unmoved. When they crossed the line, he was approached by the irate mayor, who had seen his town's big day ruined. 'We've got nothing against you,' Hinault told him. 'It's the organisers we are protesting against.'

The mayor was furious, and kept interrupting Hinault, prompting an even more angry response from the 23-year old: 'Shut your mouth!'

'If I have something to say, I'll say it!' said the mayor.

'Not when someone is speaking to you. Then you shut up.'

Hinault went on to win that Tour, and made it two the following year. In 1980

he again found himself at the centre of a controversy, when, suffering from a knee injury but in the yellow jersey, he staged a clandestine late-night exit from the Tour, heading back home to Brittany without telling anyone. The journalists, their stories out-of-date as soon as they appeared, were livid. But Hinault returned to win again in 1981 and '82, before once again being struck down by injury, allowing the young pretender, Laurent Fignon, a Renault teammate, to win.

Fignon was a precocious talent, only 22 when he claimed his first Tour. His emergence, coupled with Hinault's injury, prompted the Badger's acrimonious split with Cyrille Guimard and his exit from the Renault team. He joined one of France's most colourful entrepreneurs, Bernard Tapie, in his new La Vie Claire team.

It meant that in 1984 he went head-to-head against Fignon in the most eagerly anticipated 'battle of France' since the Anquetil-Poulidor tussles of the 1960s. But it was a little one-sided. Hinault, though as stubborn and aggressive as ever, had not returned to his physical peak, and Fignon was dominant, even laughing at Hinault as he launched a final, doomed attack on the stage to Alpe d'Huez.

But the tables turned again the following year. Now it was Fignon who was injured, and Hinault was back to his best. He cruised into a commanding lead with his young American teammate, Greg LeMond, emerging as the best of the rest. But then disaster struck. In the final metres of the 14th stage, to St Etienne, Hinault crashed heavily. His face took the brunt of it; he remounted his bike and freewheeled across the line with blood pouring from his nose, which was quickly diagnosed as broken.

For the remaining nine stages Hinault sported two black eyes: a look that suited a rider who was compared to a boxer ('the Badger needs an opponent') by his old mentor, Guimard. Then he began to suffer from bronchitis. And, by the time they reached the Pyrenees, it was clear that he was struggling.

Matters came to a head on stage 17, to Luz Ardiden, when LeMond chased down an attacker, Stephen Roche, and the two gained a gap. Behind, Hinault was falling behind. LeMond, second overall, could see that it was his chance. He asked the La Vie Claire director, Paul Köchli, for permission to cooperate. But there was a problem. Roche was a threat. If LeMond and Roche stayed away, LeMond would inherit Hinault's yellow jersey, but Roche would also leapfrog the Badger, moving into second. Köchli couldn't risk that, and told LeMond not to work.

The break was caught, and Hinault held on, just, to win his fifth Tour, tying the record with Anquetil and Merckx. But LeMond was convinced that he hadn't been told the truth about Hinault's condition on that stage to Luz Ardiden. Rather than being just 40 seconds behind him and Roche – as LeMond was told at the time – he came to believe that Hinault had been minutes behind.

To pacify LeMond, Hinault made a pledge. 'Next year,' he told him, 'it's you who'll win the Tour, and I'll be there to help you.'

It has gone down as one of the most famous – and, as it turned out, ambiguous – promises in Tour history, and it set the context for one of the most compelling and intriguing races in the event's history.

◀ **Disgrace**

Michel Pollentier relaxes after winning the Alpe d'Huez stage of the 1978 Tour de France, and claiming the yellow jersey. But not for long. When he went to dope control Pollentier was discovered trying to beat the system. He had a bulb of somebody else's urine in his armpit, and a tube taped to his body, allowing him to give a 'clean' sample. He was disqualified.

Best of France

Hinault keeps a wary eye on his former protégé, Laurent Fignon, as the two go head-to-head in the 1984 Tour. Hinault, returning from injury with his new La Vie Claire team, was not back to his best, and Fignon won easily for the second consecutive year.

End is in sight

Hinault leads the riders across the cobbled streets of Paris on the final stage of the 1978 Tour de France. On two occasions Hinault achieved the unusual feat of winning the final stage on the Champs-Élysées, in 1979 and 1982.

Adulation

Bernard Hinault is acclaimed by French fans in Paris after his first victory in 1978.

Lanterne rouge
Hinault acknowledges the *lanterne rouge*, Gerhard Schönbacher, who finished last man on general classification two years in a row, in 1979 and '80. The last rider was known as the *lanterne rouge* after the red lantern that hung on a train's final carriage.

◄ **Skittles**
A pile-up, and the disheartening sight of the peloton disappearing into the distance …

Number four ▶

Number four ▶
Hinault leads Zoetemelk and Peter Winnen
on Alpe d'Huez in 1982, en route to his
fourth Tour.

Champion

A rare show of emotion from Bernard Hinault after winning his fourth Tour title in 1982. The men beside him are Félix Lévitan, co-director of the Tour, and the then-mayor of Paris, Jacques Chirac.

The professor ▶

Laurent Fignon rides to his first Tour victory in 1983. Hinault, his Renault team leader, was missing with injury, and the 22-year old Fignon, nicknamed the professor because he briefly attended university and wore glasses, stepped into the Badger's shoes and won convincingly.

Pedalling wounded ▲

Stephen Roche pushes his Peugeot teammate Pascal Simon, in yellow, during the 1983 Tour. Simon had crashed the previous day and broken his shoulder blade, though he struggled on for seven days before abandoning, still in yellow, and in tears.

▲ **New guard**

The new guard: Scotsman Robert Millar in the polka dot jersey of King of the Mountains, and Greg LeMond, in the rainbow jersey of world champion, during the 1984 race. Millar finished fourth, the best ever placing by a British rider, with LeMond third, the best ever performance by an English-speaking cyclist.

Bloodied badger
Hinault crashed and broke his nose in St Etienne during the 1985 Tour. He
finished the Tour – and won it, for a fifth time – looking like a street fighter. But
most agreed it was a look that suited him.

Anglo invasion, 1986–90

The smiles at the top of Alpe d'Huez appeared to tell the story, and, in the TV commentary box, Greg LeMond's wife, Kathy, offered her own running account of the most extraordinary dénouement to what many agreed had been the most extraordinary Tour.

As she watched her husband, who had shadowed Bernard Hinault all the way up Alpe d'Huez, draw level with Hinault, pat him on the back and exchange a few words before both broke into wide smiles, her happiness bubbled over. 'It's fabulous!' said Kathy, her voice crackling with emotion as LeMond and Hinault joined hands in the air and rode side-by-side to the finish line. 'I'm glad to see they're just good friends now.'

For over two weeks Hinault and LeMond had waged a bitter war on the roads of France. The previous night, before their showdown on the Alpe, they had 'been at each other's throats' until four in the morning, according to Bernard Tapie, the owner of their La Vie Claire team. Because this was the strangest thing about their battle: Hinault and LeMond were teammates. They were supposed to be on the same side.

The 1986 Tour was part two of a story that began in 1985, when LeMond helped a battered and bruised Hinault to his fifth victory. LeMond felt that, in helping Hinault, he had scuppered his own chances, and Hinault appeared to recognise this. Thus he made his pledge, as the 1985 race drew to a close, to help LeMond the following season – his final one before retiring, as he had always promised, on 14 November, his 32nd birthday.

Hinault and LeMond could not have been more different. LeMond was a blond-haired, blue-eyed Californian; he was warm, friendly and engaging. He could also be fragile and insecure. Hinault, on the other hand, was anything but. Dark, handsome and gruff, Le Blaireau (the Badger) remains perhaps the most feared of all the great champions. He was the undisputed *patron*, the boss of the peloton, who could dictate what happened and when.

There was something of the old world versus new world about the 1986 Tour,

 All smiles
Hinault, LeMond and the colourful La Vie Claire team owner Bernard Tapie on the podium at Alpe d'Huez. Hinault has just won the stage, LeMond is in yellow, and Tapie is happy. But the peace doesn't last long.

with LeMond representing the growing army of English-speakers, along with the Australian Phil Anderson, the Irishmen Sean Kelly and Stephen Roche and the Scotsman Robert Millar.

Anderson told a story that summed up Hinault. Riding to Saint-Lary-Soulan during the 1981 Tour, Anderson found himself alongside Hinault, a rider he revered. 'It was a warm day and I'd noticed that the riders would be handed a drink by a spectator, and then they'd pass it to each other across the front of the peloton,' said Anderson. 'I saw someone with a frosty can of Coke by the side, so I reached out and thanked him for it as I grabbed it. I took a swig and looked across at Hinault, who was frothing at the mouth. I reached out to offer him the can of Coke and he gave me this look of disgust … And he takes a swipe and knocks it out my hands. I think he might even have growled.'

Hinault was not a man to be messed with. Neither, perhaps, was he a man to pass up on the chance of winning – especially at the Tour.

As the 1986 race got under way Hinault rode in such a way that suggested he had no intention of honouring his pledge to help LeMond. He attacked on the first day in the Pyrenees, escaping with Pedro Delgado to build a lead of more than four minutes. Behind, LeMond could not chase his teammate. And he grew increasingly frustrated as riders from other teams appeared reluctant to hunt down the Badger.

It got worse the next day. Hinault, now in the yellow jersey, did it again. He attacked alone on the descent of the Col du Tourmalet and built a huge lead, before he began to suffer. He was caught before the final climb, to Superbagnères, and seemed to have been left for dead as LeMond won the stage. But Hinault staged a miraculous recovery on the climb to hold on to the yellow jersey.

Their battle was eventually decided on the final day in the Alps, finishing at Alpe d'Huez. LeMond and Hinault arrived together at the base of the mountain. They had blown everyone else away. LeMond wore the yellow jersey of race leader for the first time in his career – the first time any American had led the Tour – having wrested it from Hinault's shoulders as the Frenchman suffered with a leg injury on the previous day's stage.

But, having fought so bitterly, a truce seemed to be called on the Alpe. Hinault led all the way, LeMond shadowing him, only drawing level when the road flattened at the top. But LeMond wasn't attacking: he patted Hinault on the back, as the great Frenchman turned and smiled. Then they clasped hands, as Hinault eased ahead to claim the stage win.

Yet it wasn't the Hollywood ending that it appeared. Later it emerged that Tapie had driven alongside the leading pair in the valley before Alpe d'Huez and instructed LeMond: 'You've won the Tour, Greg. But this is really important: let Hinault lead – it's his last Tour – and let him win the stage.'

It also transpired that Hinault had warned LeMond that he could be in danger if he attacked and dropped him. The slopes of the Alpe were packed with hundreds of thousands of spectators, most of them French, most of them wanting Hinault to win. LeMond believed he could be at risk; his mind flashed back to the 1975 Tour, when Eddy Merckx, taking on another Frenchman, Bernard Thévenet, was punched in the kidneys while climbing the Puy de Dôme. It cost Merckx the Tour.

Hinault played on LeMond's fears. Or perhaps he really did have his best interests at heart – only Hinault knows. Later, he admitted: 'I kept telling him to stay behind. There was absolutely no need for him to go and wear himself out on the climb. We were six minutes ahead. I told him, "You stay calm, don't panic, and we go to the finish together."'

When they crossed the line hand-in-hand it seemed, to everyone watching (including LeMond's wife, Kathy), that Hinault had finally conceded defeat, and that he would, for the remaining five stages, fulfil his original pledge to help LeMond. But when he appeared alongside the yellow jersey-clad LeMond on French television's daily Tour programme, held in a makeshift studio on the summit of the Alpe, Hinault reneged once more. Sipping from a bottle of beer, and with a white towel wrapped around his neck, Hinault casually remarked: 'The Tour is not finished. There could be a crash, many things can happen. [But] if we have a war, it'll be a fair war and the stronger one will win.'

As Hinault spoke, the colour drained from LeMond's face. He seemed puzzled – and no wonder. The presenter asked him if he'd need to attack Hinault. 'But I don't want to attack!' said LeMond, forcing a nervous laugh.

LeMond survived the remaining days, and a couple more Hinault attacks, to win his first Tour, and the first by an English-speaker. The following year, remarkably, there was number two, when Stephen Roche, during a season in which he won the Giro d'Italia, Tour and world championship, defeated Delgado in another close-fought, exciting tussle. It was a Tour defined by Roche's recovery on the climb to La Plagne at the end of stage 20, when he chased Delgado, in the yellow jersey, and, through the mist, appeared just behind him at the summit.

The effort caused Roche to collapse; he was given oxygen and taken to hospital but recovered to claim his only Tour.

Delgado came good the following year, but it was a victory tarnished by his positive drugs test for probenicid, a substance reportedly used as a steroid-masking agent. Though banned by the International Olympic Committee, it wasn't added to cycling's banned list until the following year. Delgado was cleared. But the general ambivalence towards drugs was illustrated in the coverage of the case, the punishment he would have suffered had he been found guilty (a ten-minute penalty), and, especially, in the reaction of his colleagues. The second-placed rider, Steven Rooks, spoke out in support of Delgado and suggested he would refuse the yellow jersey if the Spaniard was penalised. (Rooks later admitted to using testosterone, amphetamines and, after 1989, EPO during his career.)

LeMond missed both those Tours after being shot in a hunting accident in April 1987. He had been lucky to survive, but it seemed, when he returned to racing, that he would never recover full fitness and contend for another Tour. He struggled even to finish races, and almost quit the sport during the 1989 Giro d'Italia, only to suddenly come good in the final time trial, in which he was second.

He went into the 1989 Tour with his confidence returning but his ambitions limited to individual stages. And yet, with Delgado inexplicably conceding 2 minutes, 40 seconds on day one after turning up late for his prologue time trial, it became a two-horse race between two previous winners, who had both lost years to injury: LeMond and Laurent Fignon.

Fignon was stronger in the mountains, LeMond in the time trials, but, ahead of a final 24km time trial from Versailles to Paris, the Frenchman had a healthy 50 seconds' lead. It seemed enough. And yet, as they got under way, and LeMond adopted his aerodynamic tuck on his new tri-bars, the difference between the two riders was obvious. LeMond was as smooth as silk, cutting through the air like Concorde. Fignon shifted constantly on his saddle, as though he couldn't find a comfortable position. Adding to the untidy effect, his blond ponytail billowed in the wind; he cut an ugly sight (it later emerged that Fignon was suffering from a horrendous saddle sore that almost prevented him sitting on the saddle at all).

LeMond, astonishingly, overturned the 50-second advantage, beating Fignon by 58 seconds on the stage to claim the yellow jersey. It remains the smallest ever winning margin, and it came – cruelly – to define Fignon's career. In his autobiography, Fignon – who died of cancer in 2010 – recalled being asked: 'Are you the guy who lost the Tour by eight seconds?'

'No,' he would respond. 'I'm the guy who won it twice.'

'Le Tour du Nouveau Monde,' *L'Équipe* had declared the day after LeMond's first victory in 1986. But the headline was prescient to a degree that neither the paper nor anyone else connected with the sport could have predicted. With LeMond adding his third and final title in 1990, Fignon's near-miss remains the closest a Frenchman has come to winning the Tour since Hinault in 1985.

The great comeback
Perhaps the most famous time trial in Tour history: Greg LeMond overturns a 50-second deficit on Laurent Fignon to win the final stage into Paris and snatch the victory from the Frenchman's grasp.

Fignon flies

At the 1989 Tour Laurent Fignon leads the defending champion, Pedro Delgado, as they attempt to distance the man in the yellow jersey, Greg LeMond. The lead swung back and forth between Fignon and LeMond, and was never more than a minute. On the 17th stage to Alpe d'Huez, with LeMond ahead by 53 seconds, Fignon won to move into a 26-second lead, increasing that to 50 the next day to Villard-de-Lans. It seemed enough. It wasn't.

Top two

Pedro Delgado leads Stephen Roche on stage 19 of the 1987 Tour, to Villard-de-Lans. Delgado won the stage but Roche remained dangerously close.

Showing the strain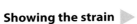

The strain shows on Roche's face as he defends his yellow jersey on the 20th stage to Alpe d'Huez. The Spaniard Marino Lejerreta sits behind him.

Tan lines

Another piece of history was made by Shelley Verses, the American soigneur
with the French Toshiba squad. Verses was believed to be the first woman to

▲ **Top table**

The three five-time Tour winners meet at the 1987 race: Eddy Merckx, Bernard
Hinault and Jacques Anquetil. Anquetil would die just four months later of

Testing times ▼

Pedro Delgado emerges from the anti-doping caravan during the 1988 Tour. Delgado was at the centre of a doping controversy when he tested positive for probenicid. But although the substance had been added to the International Olympic Committee's banned list, it was not on the International Cycling Union's banned list – yet. It was added the following year. Delgado was cleared.

Old master, young pretender

Greg LeMond, in the rainbow jersey of world champion, leads a young Miguel Indurain on their breakaway to Luz Ardiden on stage 16 of the 1990 Tour. LeMond would go on to win his third and final Tour, but Indurain, who had been Pedro Delgado's loyal domestique, would go on to win the next five.

Through the corridor ▼

The crowds throng Alpe d'Huez
in 1987 for stage 20, won by the
Spaniard Federico Echave.

Lucho the bird
The Colombian climber Luis 'Lucho' Herrera in the polka dot King of the Mountains jersey during the 1987 Tour. He was crowned King of the Mountains twice, in 1985 and 1987, but his most memorable victory was in 1984 at Alpe d'Huez, where he became the first Colombian stage winner.

Pedro fights

Pedro Delgado trying to claim time from Stephen Roche during their close battle in the 1987 Tour, which Roche eventually won by just 40 seconds.

Super van Poppel

Jean-Paul van Poppel wins his third stage of the 1988 Tour, prevailing in one of the classic sprinters' finishes in Bordeaux. Van Poppel was one of the first riders to have a team dedicated to setting him up for the sprints, and the Superconfex 'green train' was devastatingly effective.

Dutch king of the mountains
Luis Herrera leads the lanky Dutchman, Steven Rooks, as well as Pedro Delgado in yellow and Andy Hampsten, on stage 15 of the 1988 race, finishing at Luz Ardiden. Rooks would finish second to Delgado in Paris and retain the polka-dot king of the mountains jersey he is wearing here.

Anglo supremacy
Another of the English-speaking pioneers, Andy Hampsten, leads his countryman and team leader, Greg LeMond, on the climb of Superbagnères at the end of stage 13 in 1986. Hampsten was first to attack on the climb, but LeMond won the stage, inching closer to Bernard Hinault's yellow jersey.

Chiappucci in charge ▲

Greg LeMond, in the rainbow jersey of world champion, tracks the man in
yellow, Claudio Chiappucci, in the Pyrenees, on stage 16 of the 1990 Tour.
Chiappucci was the surprise package after featuring in a four-man break that
gained 10 minutes on stage one. Chiappucci ended up in yellow for eight days,
with LeMond chipping away at his lead and claiming the overall lead on the
penultimate stage for this third, and final, overall win.

Marco Pantani looks lost in his thoughts as he sits on the road during the riders' strike before stage 12 of the 1998 Tour de France. They were protesting against their treatment by the police and authorities, who raided rooms and made arrests for the possession of doping products.

A dark shadow, 1991–98

It is difficult to pinpoint precisely when the shadow first became apparent. It was never visible; you will not find any evidence of it in the photographs, though its effects could perhaps be detected by the experienced eye, in moving pictures that showed riders climbing mountains with an ease that defied previous generations.

Its effects became obvious, too, in the deaths of a number of young cyclists in the early 1990s. That – it is generally understood – is when the scourge of EPO infiltrated the peloton like a particularly virulent illness.

The picture showing Marco Pantani, sitting cross-legged on the road, might sum up the EPO era, and serve as a poignant memorial to the myths it helped create and the terrible damage it caused.

EPO is erythropoetin, a substance that stimulates the production of the oxygen-carrying red blood cells that are so essential to endurance athletes. Unlike some previously popular drugs, such as amphetamines, EPO's effects were not negligible: they could transform an athlete, turning a moderately gifted rider into a champion. But there were dangers; an increase in the concentration of red cells also thickens the blood, which led to serious health risks – perhaps even the heart attacks that led to the deaths of around 20 young cyclists in the early 1990s.

The dangers were apparent when the athlete slept: his heart slowed down, and struggled to keep the thick blood circulating. At the mid-1990s height of the EPO era, there were chilling tales of riders sleeping with heart-rate monitors attached to their chests. If their heartbeat fell below a rate deemed 'safe', they got up, went for a walk, or rode a stationary bike, to get the heart, and the blood, moving again.

The picture here of Marco Pantani, with the thousand-yard stare, lost in his own thoughts, is worth many thousands of words. What is going through his mind?

It is from the 1998 Tour de France, which he won. But the race was

One of the worst crashes in the history of the Tour occurred at Armentières in 1994. For once it didn't involve the kamikaze sprinter Djamolidine Abdoujaparov (on the left), who avoided the trouble and won. A policeman stepped out to take a photograph and Wilfried Nelissen, Laurent Jalabert and another eight riders slammed into him. Jalabert knocked out several teeth and suffered severe facial injuries.

overshadowed when, on 8 July, three days before the start, a vehicle belonging to Festina, the world's number one team, was stopped on the French-Belgian border, and found to contain an enormous stash of doping products, including EPO, human growth hormone and testosterone. The driver was the team's soigneur, Willy Voet, who was arrested and, as the Tour began, placed under formal investigation.

Initially this was a side-story, mentioned only in passing by journalists as the Tour got under way with its usual fanfare. If anything, there was more than the usual fanfare, since the Grand Départ was the first ever to be held overseas, with the prologue in Dublin and another two stages in Ireland before a ferry transfer back to France.

The Irish start was belated recognition for the two great Irish riders of the 1980s, Sean Kelly and Stephen Roche, but it was also convenient for the organisers. The

football World Cup was staged in France that summer, with the final falling on the second weekend in July – by which time the Tour would traditionally have been in full swing. Fearing that the race would be overshadowed by the World Cup, the Grand Départ was put back a week. By the time the Tour reached France, the World Cup would be over; they would have the country, and the media spotlight to themselves.

Up to a point. France won the World Cup, ensuring weeks more coverage for *Les Bleus*. And yet the Tour also received more than its usual coverage. It just wasn't the kind of coverage – on the front as well as the back pages – they would have wanted.

There were stories, perhaps apocryphal, of drugs being tossed over the side of the boat as the riders and their entourage made their way to France. Meanwhile, the soigneur at the centre of the scandal, Willy Voet, languishing in a prison cell in Lille, changed his initial explanation for his stash of drugs. He had said, improbably, that they were for his personal use. Now he admitted they were for the team, and the next day, as stage four took the riders from Plouay to Cholet, the Festina director and team doctor were suspended; both later admitted that systematic doping took place on the team. Three days later, the Festina team was expelled from the race, despite the tearful protests of innocence from its leader, Richard Virenque, who'd finished third in 1996, and second in 1997.

It didn't end there. The Dutch TVM team came under suspicion; so did the Spanish ONCE squad, and other teams and riders. There were police raids on riders' rooms at night; riders were interrogated, and some taken to hospital, where they were forced to undergo blood, urine and hair tests.

The Tour was in freefall. Not since 1904, when Henri Desgrange declared that it couldn't be held again because of the rampant cheating that went on during the second edition, had the race faced such a crisis. Again the cause was widespread, systematic cheating. And the question being asked in newspapers, and on the television news, was whether the Tour, and the sport, could survive.

The riders reacted with indignation. Despite everything that was going on, it also became a gripping race, with Pantani and the defending champion, Jan Ullrich, locked in an exciting duel, eventually won by the Italian thanks to his superior gifts in the mountains.

The riders became fed up with their treatment at the hands of the police and media; fed up with being treated like common criminals. They complained of 'violations of their human rights', and were moved to protest. The first came at the start of stage 12, in Tarascon-sur-Ariège, with a sit-down strike that delayed the start by two hours. Another followed on stage 17 in the Alps, when, after 30km, the riders stopped and removed their race numbers. Eventually, in a show of solidarity with the under-fire TVM team, they let the riders from the Dutch squad ride ahead, at funereal pace, into the finish in Aix-les-Bains. The stage was declared void.

The image of Pantani, sitting cross-legged on the road during the first protest, is arresting partly because of what came next for Il Pirata, perhaps the most exciting climber since Charly Gaul – and similarly quirky, eccentric and sensitive. The following year, while leading the Giro d'Italia with just one day remaining, Pantani was thrown off the race after a blood test indicated a higher than normal level of haematocrit. Though there was no test for EPO (which helped explain its popularity), this was invariably a sign of EPO use.

Pantani never fully recovered. Though he returned to the Tour, he couldn't get over the shame or disgrace of his expulsion from the Giro and the suspicion that surrounded him. He suffered from depression and seemed to enter a downward spiral that led eventually to his death, alone in a hotel room in Rimini on Valentine's Day, 14 February 2004. He died from acute cocaine poisoning, but the start of the decline could be traced back to his expulsion from the 1999 Giro – or perhaps to his abuse of EPO, which, it has been widely alleged, began long before that date.

The three Tours leading up to and including the 1998 race have been discredited by subsequent revelations of doping. The 1996 winner Bjarne Riis later confessed to using EPO and other drugs; the 1997 winner Ullrich was later convicted for his involvement in a blood doping ring.

The other major figure of the 1990s was the fourth rider to win five Tours, and the first to do so in consecutive years. Miguel Indurain was widely held to be a physiological freak, given his size – 1.88m, 80kg – his reportedly enormous lungs, and his ability not just to win time trials, but to annihilate the opposition in the process. His peak – and his opponents' nadir – came on stage nine of the 1992 Tour, when he won the 65km time trial around Luxembourg by three minutes, catching the two-time Tour champion, Laurent Fignon, near the finish. Fignon had started some six minutes ahead of the Spaniard. It was his greatest humiliation.

Indurain was loved in Spain, but provoked indifferent reactions elsewhere. Like the other great time triallist, Jacques Anquetil, he was a calculating rider, who owed his Tour victories to establishing an advantage in the time trials and then riding defensively in the mountains. What was remarkable was his ability, despite his size, to remain with the best climbers in their favourite terrain. But as a spectacle, watching Indurain win the Tour could be as thrilling as watching paint dry. Off-the-bike, there was little that was exciting about Indurain, either. His nickname, 'Big Mig', referred to his size, not his personality.

On the bike, between 1991 and 1995, nobody could challenge Indurain. And few professed even to know him. Though the dominant rider of his era, he was as far removed from the great *patron* of the 1980s, Bernard Hinault, as could be imagined. He was modest, unassuming, and liked and respected by his peers, but never feared. 'When he comes down for his meal, you don't even hear him move his chair,' said his Banesto teammate, Jean-François Bernard (who had also ridden with Hinault).

When, finally, Indurain met his match in the 1996 Tour, in the unlikely shape of a balding, 32-year old Dane named Bjarne Riis, he seemed to crack. The timing was unfortunate because the route that year included a stage finish in Indurain's home town of Villava, but by then he was out of contention, suffering from bronchitis, after poor weather in the first week, and struggling for form. Indurain eventually reached Paris in 11th place, and never returned.

For months afterwards there was speculation about how Indurain would respond in 1997 and there seemed little doubt that, aged just 32, he could have added to his five Tour victories. But a man who had always been aloof and easy-going had problems with the team with which he'd spent his entire career, and didn't seem to relish the prospect of change, or, for that matter, of battling younger, stronger riders.

In January 1997 he announced his retirement, reading a brief statement to the 300 journalists gathered in a hotel suite in Pamplona, and then slipping out the room without taking any questions. Thus he ended his career as quietly as he ate dinner.

Open mouthed ▶
A rare shot of Miguel Indurain in full flight. He usually appeared so calm and in control, tapping out a smooth rhythm, even on the steepest climbs. Here he leads Luc Leblanc on stage 16 of the 1994 race, his fourth victory, to Alpe d'Huez.

◀ **Big Mig**
Indurain leads the Swiss Alex Zulle on his way to his fifth consecutive Tour victory.

Le Tour en Irlande

The peloton sweeps through Cork during the Tour's visit to Ireland in 1998. British rider Chris Boardman won the prologue time trial in Dublin and had been wearing yellow on this stage, but crashed heavily and was out of the race.

Lion king

Mario Cipollini, the flamboyant Italian sprinter who – among other contributions – pioneered colour-coordinated clothing and bike when he wore the yellow jersey in 1997. Nicknamed the Lion King, Cipollini won 12 stages between 1993 and 1999.

Tour tragedy

A discreet black ribbon tied to the bike of Fabio Casertelli, the Olympic road race champion who died during the 1995 Tour. He crashed on the descent of the Portet d'Aspet and suffered fatal head wounds.

Round the bend
The peloton, with Casertelli's Motorola teammates at the front, rides at funereal pace from Tarbes to Pau, the day after the Italian's death. The stage was neutralised as Casertelli's teammates, including a young Lance Armstrong, led the peloton across the line at the finish.

The pirate

Il Pirata – the swashbuckling Marco Pantani, one of the most exciting climbers the Tour has ever seen, on his way to victory in the troubled 1998 Tour. It wouldn't be long before scandal engulfed Pantani, who was ejected from the following year's Giro for failing a blood test. Less than five years later he died from cocaine poisoning alone in a hotel room in Rimini.

Riding through trouble ▲

Pantani laid the afoundations for his victory on
the rain-soaked stage to Les Deux Alpes, where
he distanced the previous year's winner,
Jan Ullrich.

◀ **On the drops**

Pantani rides to yet another mountain top victory
at Plateau de Beille in the Pyrenees. He tackled
the climbs as though they weren't there, on the
'drops', in full race mode, sometimes overshooting
corners. Sadly, the suspicion that his exploits were
drug-fuelled hangs over some of the most thrilling
performances of the late 1990s.

▲ Wunderkind

Jan Ullrich finished second in his debut Tour in 1996, and returned to win in dominant fashion a year later. He was only 23, and most predicted he would dominate for the next decade. He never won again, placing second on five occasions, usually to Lance Armstrong. His career ended in disgrace when he was sent home from the 2006 Tour for his involvement in a blood doping ring.

Doping Dane
The 32-year old Bjarne Riis was a surprise winner in 1996. He had been a domestique to Laurent Fignon in the early years of his career, but his transformation into a Tour champion owed rather a lot, as he later admitted, to his use of performance-enhancing drugs, including EPO. He was stripped of his Tour win, but has been reinstated in the official records, with an asterisk to note that he subsequently admitted to doping.

Lance Armstrong and Marco Pantani climbing to the summit of Mont Ventoux in 2000. Both arrived at the finish together and Pantani won the stage, though Armstrong didn't contest it, offering it to the Italian as a gift. Pantani said later that he felt insulted, and a feud began between them.

The Armstrong era, 1999–2005

The Tour de France had never witnessed anything like Lance Armstrong. Nothing like his story of overcoming cancer and returning as a Tour winner; nothing like his year-in, year-out domination; nothing like his level of global stardom, which threatened at times to turn the Tour into a celebrity circus; nothing like as many American fans, who lined the French roads in their thousands; and nothing like the suspicion that surrounded him, or the hostility directed at him, which threatened at times to engulf him, and even the race.

And, of course, the Tour had never seen a seven-time winner – even if the record would only survive seven years before being erased as doping charges against Armstrong finally stuck. In October 2012 Armstrong's name was officially wiped from the records, with the US Anti-Doping Agency (USADA) outlining, in eye-watering detail, the sophisticated and systematic doping programme operated by his team, US Postal. They claimed that Armstrong's career was 'drug-fuelled from start to finish,' and that his winning streak at the Tour amounted to 'the greatest heist sport has ever seen.'

It makes little sense to talk of alternative winners in this period, as so many of Armstrong's rivals, including every runner-up, would come under suspicion of doping or be implicated in drugs scandals. Indeed, the Tour itself requested that the titles not be reassigned and the International Cycling Union agreed, which means that there are now three official breaks in the Tour's history: world wars one and two, and Lance Armstrong.

And yet the reality is that Armstrong, even stripped of his titles, remains the dominant figure of the era. His record can be airbrushed from history but the memories of him cannot be so easily erased.

He remains the dominant figure, only now he serves as the most potent reminder of all that was allowed to go wrong with the sport in the 'EPO era.' By the time of his seventh victory in 2005, he seemed to have achieved the impossible: he had outgrown the Tour. He was no longer merely a cyclist; he was a global figure on a par with Tiger Woods, Michael Jordan and David Beckham. The father of the Tour, Henri Desgrange, who preferred his worker-

cyclists to be humble and to know their place, would have been spinning in his grave.

As his reign as champion extended into its third, fourth, fifth and sixth years, Armstrong also became even more controversial than Henri Pélissier, the 1923 winner who caused Desgrange so much trouble.

Armstrong's powers grew the more Tours he won and the more enemies he amassed. In a similar way to Bernard Hinault, he relished conflict. But with Armstrong it went further: he needed it. Opponents and their criticism did not detract from his efforts: everything provided fuel. But his rivals on the road were no match for the Texan, with his toughest opponents – those who engaged in the longest-running and most bitter battles with Armstrong – to be found not in the peloton, but in the press room.

This – the paucity of rivals and hostility of some in the media – reached its apotheosis in 2005. On the eve of his 'final' Tour, Armstrong arrived for his pre-race press conference in a cocoon of press officers, team staff, bodyguards and his rock star girlfriend, Sheryl Crow. A thousand journalists sat before him, while he sat behind the stage and fixed each inquisitor with his piercing pale blue eyes. The atmosphere was charged.

Later that day, the only rider ever to offer a serious challenge, Jan Ullrich, who pushed Armstrong close in 2003, arrived for his press conference. The German, the Tour winner in 1997, shuffled in wearing his team tracksuit and sporting a black eye. He had been out training behind his team car that morning; when the car suddenly braked, Ullrich slammed into the rear windscreen.

That such a thing might have happened to Armstrong was unimaginable. He appeared so in control that he was immune to events, such as punctures and crashes, that should be routine hazards for Tour riders; it is one curious aspect of Armstrong's reign that cannot be explained by drugs, at least not directly.

Only in one Tour, in 2003, did Ullrich seem to have Armstrong on the ropes. He beat him in the first long time trial, then, on a later stage, Armstrong had to take evasive action by riding across a field when the Spanish rider, Joseba Beloki, crashed in front of him. And finally he did crash, after catching a spectator's bag with his handlebars on the climb of Luz Ardiden. Yet Armstrong's reaction to this setback was typical: he jumped back on his bike, caught Ullrich, then immediately attacked and won the stage to all but seal his record-equalling fifth Tour victory.

On the opening day of the 2005 Tour the bruised and black-eyed Ullrich began the first stage, a longer-than-usual 19km time trial, a minute in front of Armstrong. Ullrich was a strong time triallist. But Armstrong served up the ultimate humiliation by catching him. It was a demonstration of Armstrong's superior physical condition, and, more importantly, a psychological blow from which Ullrich could not recover. After 19km, the Tour was as good as over.

Armstrong was a precocious talent in his early years, winning a stage of his first Tour in 1993, then taking an emotional victory in 1995, three days after the death of his Motorola teammate Fabio Casartelli, when he crossed the line in Limoges, his eyes directed and fingers pointing towards the heavens. In those days Armstrong's wins came on tough, undulating days, but he struggled in the high mountains, where the yellow jersey is won and lost. He did not look like a rider who would ever be capable of winning the Tour de France.

Then, in 1996, he was cut down in his prime, announcing as the season wound down that he had raced for most of the year (and won a tough classic, Flèche Wallonne) with testicular cancer. Within days he learned that it had spread to his lungs, abdomen and brain. Yet, as he would later relate in excruciating detail in his multimillion-selling book, *It's Not About the Bike*, Armstrong refused to yield and fought the disease with all he had, seeking a range of experts and opinions.

His return, at the start of the 1998 season, was slow at first, and there were setbacks. But at the end of the year he was fourth in the Tour of Spain: his first high placing in one of the three-week Grand Tours. The main difference between the pre- and post-cancer Armstrong seemed to be that he was now able to perform in the high mountains, a difference he put down to upper body weight loss.

His performance in Spain meant that Armstrong began the 1999 Tour de France as an outsider. But he was a popular outsider; his story resonated with the Tour director, Jean-Marie Leblanc, who craved positive publicity just twelve months after the Festina doping scandal left the Tour on its knees. As in 1968, the year after Tom Simpson's death on Mont Ventoux, a fresh start was required. And so when Armstrong won the prologue time trial in The Vendée, Leblanc spoke for many: 'This is the Tour of renewal, of a return to the top level, and look at [Armstrong]: he incarnates that.'

Towards the end of the 1999 Tour it emerged that Armstrong had tested positive after this prologue, for cortisone. When a French newspaper got hold of this information, Armstrong called a press conference. 'I made a mistake in taking something I didn't consider to be a drug,' he said. He explained that he had used a cream containing cortisone to treat a saddle sore – an excuse accepted by the authorities when he produced a prescription for the drug, though the note should have been produced before, not after.

At the time, it was a side-story to the dominant narrative: the extraordinary Armstrong comeback. Most wanted to believe in Armstrong. Post-Festina, the Tour needed to believe in Armstrong. Yet the doping rumours would not go away, especially when it was revealed in 2001 that he was working with a notorious Italian doctor, Michele Ferrari. When he learned of Armstrong's involvement with Ferrari, the other American Tour winner, Greg LeMond, remarked: 'If Armstrong's clean, it's the greatest comeback. And if he's not, then it's the greatest fraud.'

Though Armstrong maintained that he never used illegal performance enhancing drugs, such controversies would come to define his career almost as much as his performances, which were phenomenal – though we now know how: with the help of a cocktail of banned drugs, including EPO and then, when a test was developed, blood transfusions.

His strategy was to rely on a simple tactic, of attacking hard on the first or toughest day in the high mountains to hammer home his superiority. Then, with Armstrong in yellow, his team, US Postal, would control the race to an extent rarely seen, as though they were a mere extension to their dominant leader. As in the case of their leader, their superiority can now be explained by the systematic doping confirmed by the US Anti-Doping Agency.

Two of Armstrong's most memorable performances came on Alpe d'Huez. In 2001 the stage included the Col du Glandon and Col de la Madeleine before the Alpe, and, on both climbs, Armstrong appeared in difficulty. For once he and his team did not ride at the front. Instead, he grimaced in apparent agony as the pace was set by Ullrich's Telekom troops, who, in turn, appeared to gain encouragement from seeing Armstrong suffer. Thus they rode even harder.

By the time they reached Alpe d'Huez, they were flagging. But Armstrong had been bluffing; it had been 'a game of poker,' he said later. At the foot of the Alpe he rode to the front of the group, looked Ullrich in the eye – 'The Look' as it was dubbed – and then attacked. He rode alone up the mountain to win the stage, taking almost two minutes out of the second-placed Ullrich.

The second occasion was in 2004. The organisers had laid on one of the most audacious stages in Tour history: an individual time trial up Alpe d'Huez. For the fans this was a treat: they would see each rider struggle alone up the mountain; the entertainment would last virtually all day. And they responded enthusiastically – estimates of the numbers who packed the slopes that day range from 500,000 to (more fancifully, perhaps) a million. There were reports of fans camping out for a week to reserve the best vantage points on the steep, snaking 14.5km climb, with its 21 hairpin bends.

It was certainly mobbed. But there were echoes of 1986, when LeMond feared for his safety in the midst of his battle for the yellow jersey with Bernard Hinault. On that occasion the American spent the entire climb in Hinault's shadow, with the great Frenchman playing on LeMond's anxiety by suggesting he might be in danger if he attacked and rode up alone. In 2004, however, Armstrong had no choice: it was an individual time trial. He would be alone, exposed and, potentially, vulnerable.

It was later claimed that, just before he set out on his ride, Armstrong received a death threat, which the police took seriously enough to place snipers in the vehicles that preceded and followed him. That is shocking, of course, but so was the very idea that he might have been the victim of any kind of attack. Save for one crazed fan punching Eddy Merckx in 1975, there was no history of violence in the Tour; it had simply never been part of the sport's culture.

Armstrong was not phyisically attacked, but his ride up the Alpe was not without incident. While he was cheered and encouraged by most, there were boos and jeers from a few. When he crossed the line, he was covered in spit – not all his own. Naturally, he appeared undeterred, carving a line through the thick mass of spectators, who crowded into the road, and he won the stage by over a minute from Ullrich. But he admitted that it had been 'scary. There were too many people, a lot of Germans, a lot of Belgians, who weren't being too nice.' His reaction, however, was typical. 'It motivates me more than anything,' he said of the abuse. 'It certainly doesn't work against me … it puts a little fuel on the fire.'

He was similarly defiant when, eight years later, USADA charged him with doping, Armstrong's response was to undermine their authority and dismiss their 'heinous' pursuit of him, which he characterised as 'a witchhunt.'

A few days later, at a cancer conference in Montreal, he took to the stage. 'Well, good morning,' he said. 'I thought in light of recent events I ought to re-introduce myself. My name is Lance Armstrong. I'm a cancer survivor … And yes, I won the Tour de France seven times.'

Yet now, according to the official records, he didn't. Some of the more unsavoury details in the USADA report included Armstrong's intimidation of riders who spoke out against doping, such as Christophe Bassons, and his efforts to coerce teammates to 'get with the (doping) programme,' or get off the team.

The picture painted of Armstrong in this 1,000-page report could hardly have been less flattering, or his fall from grace less dramatic. And yet, from Armstrong's overlooked cortisone positive in 1999, to the apparent unwillingness of those in authority to probe too deeply into exactly how he was transformed from one-day Classics specialist to record Tour winner, or into the suspicions that surrounded his team from the early 2000s, the sport cannot absolve itself of blame.

The Armstrong myth was perpetuated year after year by the Tour de France, as it welcomed the influx of American fans, the blue chip sponsors and Hollywood stars. It helped create a monster; a monster that in the end did untold harm to the integrity of the Tour, with the damage only beginning to be repaired as the 100th edition of the race gets underway in Corsica.

The Armstrong legacy was borne out by the anomalous statistic on the eve of this milestone: 99 Tours; 92 winners. The Armstrong era should perhaps be re-named the Asterisk era.

Giving chase ▶

Armstrong climbing Hautacam during the 2000 Tour. Once again his strategy was to gain time on the first day of climbing, as this was, but he didn't win the stage, with the Spaniard Javier Otxoa holding on. Just seven months later Otxoa was hit by a car while training with his twin brother Ricardo. Ricardo was killed, Javier was in a coma for 10 weeks. Although he didn't return to the sport, he won a silver medal in the road cycling event at the Athens Paralympics in 2004.

The new patron
Armstrong cruises along in the peloton during stage 13 of the 2000 Tour in the heart of Provence, from Avignon to Draguignan.

Strength in numbers ▽
Armstrong's US Postal team doing what it did best: riding en masse at the front in defence of Armstrong's yellow jersey.

Richard Virenque, who was at the centre of the Festina drugs scandal in 1998, returned and won several stages, including Mont Ventoux in 2002. Virenque's 1999 autobiography, *Ma Vérité* (My Truth), protested his innocence, but a year later he broke down at the trial in Lille into the affair, and tearfully admitted to doping, even as he insisted – improbably – that it was unintentional. He was banned for nine months.

◀ **Lance almost blows it**

Armstrong climbs towards Morzine on stage 16 of the 2000 Tour, en route to his second victory. It was a Tour in which he won only one stage, the long time trial three days before Paris, but he had been determined to prove that 1999 hadn't been a one-off, and that even with Jan Ullrich and Marco Pantani in the field, he could win. This, though, was his toughest day. He 'blew' on the final climb and Ullrich dropped him after Pantani had set the race alight with his own suicide attack.

Crash!
Chaos on stage five of the 2002 Tour, from
Soissons to Rouen, as riders untangle
themselves after a mass pile-up.

Mayhem on the Alpe
Armstrong battles through crowds estimated at half a million during the Alpe d'Huez time trial in the 2004 Tour. After he received a death threat before the stage it was reported that police snipers accompanied him in vehicles in front and behind.

▲ **Once masters**

ONCE, the Spanish team, in the team time trial from Joinville to Saint-Dizier. They were masters at this discipline, and at much else besides, winning virtually everywhere. But the 'yellow peril,' as they were dubbed, never won the yellow jersey at the Tour.

Armstrong felled
Perhaps the single most dramatic moment of the Armstrong era: he catches his
handlebars in a spectator's bag, falls off, while Ullrich takes evasive action, then

Shadowing Jan

Ullrich, Armstrong, Haimar Zubeldia and Ivan Basso on the Col du Peyresourde during stage 14 of the 2003 race.

No gifts

'Pas de cadeaux' – no gifts. That was the advice from Bernard Hinault to Lance Armstrong, whom the Badger thought had gifted too many stages to rivals, including Pantani in 2000. He didn't at Le Grand Bornand, outsprinting Andreas Kloden for one of his five stage wins in 2004.

No butts
Anatomy of a bunch sprint. While Tom Boonen in the green jersey wins, Robbie McEwen uses his head to try and beat fellow Australian Stuart O'Grady at the end of stage 3 of the 2005 Tour in Tours.

In the pink
A recent phenomenon has been for the Tour to attract bigger crowds when it leaves France. Here the peloton is led by German superteam T-Mobile during the 2005 race, during a stage that finished just across the French-German border in Karlsruhe.

Plucky Tommy

Thomas Voeckler, the French darling of the 2004 Tour, bravely defends his yellow jersey on the Pyrenean climb to Plateau de Beille, which he held on to for an improbable 10 days.

Pirate's last stand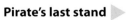

The late Marco Pantani, one of the sport's greatest ever climbers, doing what he did best during stage 16 of the 2000 Tour to Morzine. Angered by Armstrong's gift of the Mont Ventoux stage four days earlier, he had won the previous day to Courchavel, and went on a suicide attack to Morzine. He put Armstrong in difficulty but also destroyed himself, and didn't finish the Tour.

◄ **Millar time**
David Millar, riding his first Tour de France in 2000, beat Lance Armstrong to win the opening time trial and claim the yellow jersey. He became only the fourth British rider to lead the Tour.

Full throttle
Three of the top sprinters of the late 1990s: Mario
Cipollini, Tom Steels and Erik Zabel battle it out.

The Armstrong era 1999–2005 **201**

Mr Clean

Christophe Bassons, a French rider who had refused to take part in Festina's
doping programme when with that team, earned notoriety at the 1999
Tour through his newspaper column in *Le Parisien*, in which he cast doubt
on whether the sport was cleaner post-Festina. On one stage, said Bassons,
Armstrong "grabbed me by the shoulder, because he knew that everyone
would be watching, and he knew that at that moment, he could show everyone
that he was the boss. He stopped me, and he said what I was saying wasn't true,
what I was saying was bad for cycling, that I mustn't say it, that I had no right to
be a professional cyclist, that I should quit cycling, that I should quit the Tour,
and finished by saying 'F*** you.'"

▲ Intimidation

These pictures show the infamous day in 2004 when Lance Armstrong chased down Filippo Simeoni, a lowly Italian who presented no threat to Armstrong's bid to win his sixth Tour. Simeoni had testified against Armstrong's coach, Michele Ferrari, saying he had prescribed him human growth hormone and EPO. By chasing him down, Armstrong forced his overall rivals to chase, thus sabotaging Simeoni's effort to win the stage. After they returned to the peloton, Armstrong made a zip-the-lips gesture.

Starting to crack ▷
Stage 16 of the 2006 Tour, with the yellow jersey, Floyd Landis, eighth in line.
He cracked on the final climb to La Toussuire to lose the lead but bounced
back next day to win in Morzine after one of the greatest solo attacks in Tour
history but which was later exposed as a sham.

Aussie and British rules, 2006–12

When Lance Armstrong retired from cycling after winning his seventh Tour in 2005, he addressed the crowds on the Champs-Élysées. He was defiant and aimed his parting shot at those who suspected him of doping: 'To all the cynics, I'm sorry for you … You need to believe in these riders. I'm sorry you can't dream big and I'm sorry you don't believe in miracles.'

But it was difficult to dream big, or to believe in miracles, when, the following year, the Tour began against the backdrop of the biggest doping scandal since Festina in 1998. Operacion Puerto uncovered an international blood doping ring, run by a doctor in Madrid, which implicated Armstrong's old rivals, and the two favourites for the 2006 race, Ivan Basso and Jan Ullrich. Both were expelled on the eve of a Tour eventually won by Floyd Landis. But four days later Landis was stripped of the title after testing positive for testosterone.

In 2007, after a spectacular Grand Départ in London, the race looked to be wrapped up by Michael Rasmussen until, in the final week, it emerged that he had misled the authorities over his whereabouts, allegedly to avoid drugs tests. He was sent home and the race was won by Alberto Contador, who had missed the 2006 race because his team, Astana, was so heavily involved in Operacion Puerto and expelled. By this point, the sport was so mired in doping scandals that it was difficult to know where to look; there appeared to be no shafts of light; the sport was shrouded in darkness.

It continued in 2008, when there were positive tests for stage winners Riccardo Riccò, Stefan Schumacher, Leonardo Piepoli and the King of the Mountains, Bernhard Kohl. But there was also a new star, Mark Cavendish, who announced his arrival as the world's fastest sprinter by winning four stages. Riccò had been sent home before the 12th stage, which would give Cavendish his third win, and at the finish in Narbonne the sprinter from the Isle of Man was asked about the latest scandal. He paused for 20 seconds before answering: 'I just don't think Riccardo Riccò loves the sport like I do.'

By now the UCI, cycling's world governing body, seemed to be finally waking up to the problem, and even tacitly acknowledging that little, if anything,

seemed to have changed since the Festina scandal. They introduced 'biological passports' to track the riders' blood and hormonal values over time; abnormal fluctuations could result in a doping sanction, even if there was no positive test. The fact that riders were being caught and punished – unheard of previously – was seen as a sign of progress.

Then, in 2009, Armstrong returned. He had apparently been encouraged by the 2008 Tour, won by the relatively unheralded Carlos Sastre of Spain, to think that he could come back and win an eighth title. But Contador was also back in 2009. And, what's more, he was a teammate of Armstrong's at Astana.

It was billed as a rerun of the 1986 Tour, when Bernard Hinault and Greg LeMond went head-to-head, despite being teammates. But the now 38-year old Armstrong was not at the same level as Hinault in 1986. He was also a shadow of the old Armstrong, and incapable, except for one or two flourishes, of matching the Spaniard, who notched up his second Tour. Armstrong had to be content with third overall, with Andy Schleck second.

In fourth place, meanwhile, was the revelation. Another British rider, Bradley Wiggins, had won two gold medals on the track at the previous year's Olympics in Beijing, yet here he was at the Tour, with Garmin, a team that had entered the sport the previous year determined to fly the flag for clean sport. They were the shaft of light: the first team with anti-doping as their raison d'être, and in Wiggins they seemed to have unearthed a hidden gem. He was also a shadow of his previous self in one respect, having lost so much weight that he was almost unrecognisable from the track cyclist of old. But the result was impressive: he was matching Contador and Schleck on most of the climbs.

Contador and Schleck again went head-to-head in 2010, though their battle lacked the edge of previous great rivalries. Even when Schleck shipped his chain as he attacked in the Pyrenees, and Contador appeared to take advantage of his misfortune, prompting Schleck to say at the finish that he had 'anger in my stomach,' the froideur between them lasted a matter of hours. Indeed, the cosy nature of their rivalry was summed up by their showdown on the Col du Tourmalet, where they rode up side-by-side, neither willing – or perhaps able – to really take the other on.

Contador was crowned winner, but two months later it emerged that he had tested positive for clenbuterol. The case dragged on, eventually being resolved in early 2012 with a suspension for Contador and the loss of his 2010 crown, which passed to Schleck.

The doping problem, it was clear, had still not been resolved. The sport was not out of the woods yet. Armstrong's lambasting of the 'cynics and sceptics' in 2005 had grabbed the headlines, but only the most naive of fans could now argue that the cynics and sceptics did not have a point. This would eventually be confirmed, of course, in August 2012, when Armstrong was charged by the US Anti-Doping Agency with doping offences and stripped of his seven Tour titles.

Yet there were grounds for optimism, too. The fact that riders were being caught and punished was new, and although that brought negative headlines, it was a welcome development. As David Millar, who served a doping suspension but returned to the sport in 2006 determined to recast himself an anti-drugs campaigner, put it: 'You can't change such an ingrained culture overnight. It's going to take years. And that means positive tests for the next decade.'

If the 2010 race was another that would go down with an asterisk next to it, the following year heralded a new kind of winner. Cadel Evans, a former mountain biking prodigy, had waited years for his chance to ride the Tour, and, when it came, he applied himself to the task with dogged persistence. He was fifth in 2006, then second in 2007 and 2008, before riding poorly in 2009 and then suffering a hairline fracture of the elbow while in the yellow jersey in 2010.

By 2011 he was 34. It seemed that his chance had gone. Yet his dogged persistence served him well. In a race in which the climbers seemed below-par – with Contador not at his best after winning the Giro d'Italia, and Schleck reluctant to grab the race by the throat – Evans remained in contention by hanging on for grim death.

The pivotal moment came in the Alps, on a stage that finished at the summit of the Col du Galibier. Schleck had flown, finally. The Luxembourger, on the penultimate mountain stage, attacked early and rode to an epic stage victory. Behind him, nobody seemed willing to take up the chase. Evans was isolated, his BMC teammates all having been dropped. It was up to him, and him alone. It was now or never.

It was painful rather than pretty to watch as Evans went to the front of the small chase group, gritted his teeth, and ground his way up the climb in pursuit of the more graceful, fluid Schleck. While Schleck won the stage, Evans did enough to heave himself back into contention. And he remained well placed after the following day's stage to Alpe d'Huez, where Schleck inherited the yellow jersey from Thomas Voeckler. All that remained was a time trial in Grenoble on the penultimate day, and it was a fairly routine task for Evans to overhaul both Schleck brothers, Andy and Frank, to become the first Australian winner of the Tour de France.

One rider who might have been in contention for that Tour was Wiggins, but he crashed out, breaking his collarbone, in the first week. He had struggled in 2010, leading his new British squad, Team Sky, to follow his fourth place in 2009, and many had written him off as a Tour contender. But on the eve of the 2011 race he won the Critérium du Dauphiné: he seeemed to be back, until the crash, and the broken collarbone.

Sitting at home, nursing his injury, Wiggins watched the 2011 race unfold. 'I watched the last 10 days of that Tour de France, sitting on the sofa with my broken collarbone, as a fan,' said Wiggins later. 'It was brilliant. I was just loving it.' What he particularly admired was the way that Evans ground out the win; and he took inspiration from it. They are similar kinds of rider: strong rouleurs rather than lightweight and explosive climbers in the mould of a Contador or a Schleck. Wiggins could see that Evans' win owed as much to his sheer bloody-minded persistence, and his absolute refusal to give up, and the penny dropped: you didn't need to be the best climber in the race; it could be possible for him to win the Tour by riding cleverly, consistently, and taking full advantage of his main strength – the time trials.

When Wiggins returned, at the Tour of Spain that autumn, he was third – his first podium finish in a Grand Tour, and yet he was disappointed. He was now training as never before, following the scientific programme beloved of Team Sky and its principal, Dave Brailsford. When Brailsford launched Britain's biggest ever team in 2010, and stated that their aim was to 'win the Tour de France in the next five years with a clean British rider,' many scoffed. But now, with another Sky rider, Chris Froome, second, and Wiggins third in the Vuelta, it began to look possible.

Yet the best placing a British rider had ever achieved was fourth, first by the maverick Scotsman Robert Millar in 1984, before being repeated by Wiggins in 2009. In both cases they were close to the podium, but a long way from winning. Which meant that, when Brailsford went public with his ambition of winning, some might have laughed, but most scratched their heads in bafflement.

Brailsford was already acclaimed for having helped transform Britain's track cycling team, from laughing stock to best in the world, capped by their seven gold medals in the velodrome at the Beijing Olympics. But track cycling was the sport's poor relation; road racing was a completely different beast. British success in this discipline had proved as elusive as the Loch Ness Monster.

Their debut season, in 2010, vindicated the doubters. Brailsford would later describe that year's Tour, in which Wiggins struggled to 24th, as 'humiliating.' Later he reflected: 'For Brad as an individual, and for us as a team, certainly for myself, the suffering in 2010 was agonising. It was a horrendous experience and from that we sat down and said: "Let's not do that again; we'll move on"'.

Wiggins began the 2012 Tour as favourite. Contador was suspended, Andy Schleck was missing with injury and Evans seemed below-par. Wiggins, on the other hand, had won Paris-Nice, the Tour de Romandie and also defended his Critérium du Dauphiné title. He was the dominant stage racer, and at his side was Froome, returning from illness, and coming back into form.

He claimed the yellow jersey a week into the race, on the first hilltop finish at La Planche des Belles Filles. It owed much to Sky's organisation: they massed at the front and executed a plan designed to use their resources to maximum effect, leaving Froome and Wiggins alone at the summit. As strong riders were shed from the lead group, the only riders with them were Evans and Vincenzo Nibali, and Froome outsprinted the defending champion to win the stage.

With Wiggins consolidating his advantage in the time trial two days later, the drama came on stage 11, to La Toussuirre, when Froome momentarily dropped his leader. They had reeled in Nibali, but Wiggins only seemed in trouble when his teammate accelerated. Froome was riding away, but an instruction came over his earpiece: 'You better have a good reason to be attacking. If not, wait for Brad.'

He waited for Wiggins, but it sparked the main debate of the 2012 race: was Froome stronger than Wiggins in the mountains? It was a replay not of the great 1986 race, when the teammates Hinault and LeMond battled each other, but 1985, when Hinault was in yellow and the young pretender, LeMond, was his strongest opponent. On that occasion Hinault promised to return the following year and help the American – a pledge that would prove to be highly contentious. History was repeated, to some extent, in 2012, with Wiggins promising to come back and help Froome – though without specifying when.

With a commanding victory in the final time trial, on the penultimate day, Wiggins was acclaimed as a deserving and popular champion, and, like Evans, a history-maker. Brailsford had achieved his aim: a first British winner of the Tour, and in three years rather than five.

The other aspect of that task was even more important: the question of whether the victory was achieved legally, without drugs. Wiggins was quizzed on the subject throughout his time in yellow, not so much because there was suspicion around him, but because of the suspicion that now, understandably, clung to whoever happened to be in yellow. Initially he was annoyed at the questions about doping, railing against those who spread rumours and innuendo, particularly via the internet and Twitter, and peppering his tirade with some choice words.

But after a few days' reflection he returned to the subject, bringing it up himself. 'I am aware that there is suspicion, which I realise isn't necessarily personal but mainly a legacy of the sport's past. It's very upsetting to find myself in a position of having to defend myself. But I know about the sport's past and so I recognise that I should make my position absolutely clear. I can say, categorically, that drugs form no part of my or my team's preparation. I have always been anti-doping; I have never used a banned, performance-enhancing substance and never will.'

The Tour de France needed to hear that, and to believe it, far more than it needed a first British winner.

Hollow victory

Michael Rasmussen celebrates his stage win at the summit of the Col d'Aubisque in the yellow jersey. Hours later, he was thrown off the race by his Rabobank team for anti-doping infringements.

Upwards ▶

The Col d'Iseran featured on stage nine
of the 2007 Tour, eventually won by the
Colombian Mauricio Soler, who also ended
the Tour as King of the Mountains. Sadly,
in 2011 Soler had a terrible, 80kph crash
during the Tour of Switzerland and sustained
serious head injuries. A year later, he
announced his retirement from the sport.

Chapeau

Alberto Contador celebrates his first Tour win, taking
the yellow jersey after Michael Rasmussen's expulsion in
another race that was marred by doping scandals, with
members of the Garde Républicaine, who provide the
motorcycle escort for the Tour, even on foreign roads.

Cav comes good

Mark Cavendish, in the centre, sprints to his first stage win in Chateauroux in 2008. The French national champion Nicolas Vogondy, in the foreground, was the last survivor of a long breakaway, and was caught just before the line.

Make that two

Cavendish celebrates stage win number two in the rain in Toulouse. He won two more stages before abandoning.

The greatest?

Cavendish wins one of his six stages in 2009, this one his third, at the end of the tenth stage to Issoudun. By 2012, with 23 stage wins in six starts, he was acclaimed by *L'Equipe* as the greatest sprinter the sport had ever seen.

Top trio

Andy Schleck beats Alberto Contador to the summit of Mont Ventoux on the penultimate day of the 2009 Tour, with Lance Armstrong appearing over the brow of the hill. These three would stand on the podium in Paris next day, with Contador, already celebrating as he crosses the line, on the top step in yellow.

Chaingate

The infamous 'chaingate' incident, when Andy Schleck attacked on the Port de Balès on stage 15 in 2010 but shipped his chain as he moved clear. Behind him is Alexandre Vinokourov, with Alberto Contador moving up quickly behind his Astana teammate and about to fly past Schleck, later claiming that he hadn't realised he had a problem with his bike.

Compact

The peloton sweeps through Belgium at the start of the 2010 Tour, with stage one taking the riders from Rotterdam to Brussels.

Schleck roars ▶

Andy Schleck, after one of the epic mountain escapes, wins at the summit of the Col du Galibier on stage 18 of the 2011 Tour.

Blanket finish ▲

Mark Cavendish, with his trademark low-slung sprinting style, is on the far left
and on his way to one of his best wins at the top of a small climb in Brittany, at
Cap Frehel, ahead of Philippe Gilbert, in the black Belgian champion's jersey
and, in yellow, Thor Hushovd.

On the brink
Cadel Evans is comforted by fans after stage 19 of the 2011 race, to Alpe d'Huez.

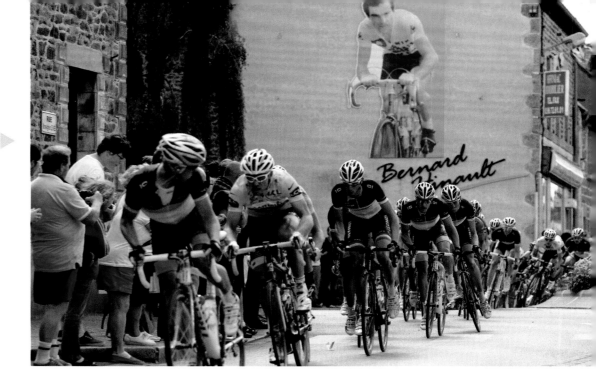

Badger looks on

The peloton races through Yffiniac, Bernard Hinault's home town in Brittany, in 2011. The world champion Thor Hushovd is the man in yellow, surrounded by members of the Leopard Trek team.

Grinding it out

Cadel Evans leads Thomas Voeckler, in yellow, on the Col du Galibier, in pursuit of Andy Schleck, on stage 18 of the 2011 Tour. It is Evans' tenacity here that will arguably win him the Tour.

The history men

Bradley Wiggins, in yellow, leads Mark Cavendish, in the rainbow jersey of world champion, on the final stage of the 2012 Tour. The two Brits were Sky teammates, with Cavendish winning three stages to add to Wiggins' overall victory.

Total supremacy
Bradley Wiggins, following in the tradition of Jacques Anquetil and his boyhood idol, Miguel Indurain, won both long races against the clock in 2012, allowing him to build a lead that he was able to defend in the mountains. Here he is in the first one in Besançon.

Team politics
Chris Froome leads his teammate Bradley Wiggins at the end of stage 17 to Peyragudes in the Pyrenees. The dynamics between the pair added tension and drama to the final week of the 2012 race. And on this, the final mountain stage, Froome looked the stronger climber, as he had also done in the Alps. He was under team orders not to leave Wiggins, leaving the question hanging: could he have won?

Titans of the Tour

The elite group of riders who have won the Tour de France more than once.

Rank	Rider	Country	Titles	Year
1	Jacques Anquetil	FRA	5	1957, 1961, 1962, 1963, 1964
2	Eddy Merckx	BEL	5	1969, 1970, 1971, 1972, 1974
3	Bernard Hinault	FRA	5	1978, 1979, 1981, 1982, 1985
4	Miguel Indurain	ESP	5	1991, 1992, 1993, 1994, 1995
5	Louison Bobet	FRA	3	1953, 1954, 1955
6	Greg LeMond	USA	3	1986, 1989, 1990
7	Philippe Thys	BEL	3	1913, 1914, 1920
8	Gino Bartali	ITA	2	1938, 1948
9	Ottavio Bottecchia	ITA	2	1924, 1925
10	Alberto Contador	ESP	2	2007, 2009
11	Fausto Coppi	ITA	2	1949, 1952
12	Laurent Fignon	FRA	2	1983, 1984
13	Nicolas Frantz	LUX	2	1927, 1928
14	Firmin Lambot	BEL	2	1919, 1922
15	André Leducq	FRA	2	1930, 1932
16	Sylvère Maes	BEL	2	1936, 1939
17	Antonin Magne	FRA	2	1931, 1934
18	Lucien Petit-Breton	FRA	2	1907, 1908
19	Bernard Thévenet	FRA	2	1975, 1977

Tour greats
1 Jacques Anquetil
2 Eddy Merckx
3 Bernard Hinault
4 Miguel Indurain
5 Philippe Thys
6 Louison Bobet
7 Greg LeMond

Tour de France winners 1903–2012

Tour	Year	Overall	Points	Mountains	Youth
1	1903	Maurice Garin			
2	1904	Henri Cornet			
3	1905	Louis Trousselier			
4	1906	René Pottier			
5	1907	Lucien Petit-Breton			
6	1908	Lucien Petit-Breton (2)			
7	1909	François Faber			
8	1910	Octave Lapize			
9	1911	Gustave Garrigou			
10	1912	Odile Defraye			
11	1913	Philippe Thys			
12	1914	Philippe Thys (2)			
13	1919	Firmin Lambot			
14	1920	Philippe Thys (3)			
15	1921	Léon Scieur			
16	1922	Firmin Lambot (2)			
17	1923	Henri Pélissier			
18	1924	Ottavio Bottecchia			
19	1925	Ottavio Bottecchia (2)			
20	1926	Lucien Buysse			
21	1927	Nicolas Frantz			
22	1928	Nicolas Frantz (2)			
23	1929	Maurice De Waele			
24	1930	André Leducq			
25	1931	Antonin Magne			
26	1932	André Leducq (2)			
27	1933	Georges Speicher		Vicente Trueba	
28	1934	Antonin Magne (2)		René Vietto	
29	1935	Romain Maes		Félicien Vervaecke	
30	1936	Sylvère Maes		Julián Berrendero	
31	1937	Roger Lapébie		Félicien Vervaecke (2)	
32	1938	Gino Bartali		Gino Bartali	
33	1939	Sylvère Maes (2)		Sylvère Maes	
34	1947	Jean Robic		Pierre Brambilla	
35	1948	Gino Bartali (2)		Gino Bartali (2)	
36	1949	Fausto Coppi		Fausto Coppi	
37	1950	Ferdinand Kübler		Louison Bobet	
38	1951	Hugo Koblet		Raphaël Géminiani	
39	1952	Fausto Coppi (2)		Fausto Coppi (2)	
40	1953	Louison Bobet	Fritz Schär	Jesús Loroño	
41	1954	Louison Bobet (2)	Ferdinand Kübler	Federico Bahamontes	
42	1955	Louison Bobet (3)	Stan Ockers	Charly Gaul	
43	1956	Roger Walkowiak	Stan Ockers (2)	Charly Gaul (2)	
44	1957	Jacques Anquetil	Jean Forestier	Gastone Nencini	
45	1958	Charly Gaul	Jean Graczyk	Federico Bahamontes (2)	
46	1959	Federico Bahamontes	André Darrigade	Federico Bahamontes (3)	
47	1960	Gastone Nencini	Jean Graczyk (2)	Imerio Massignan	

48	1961	Jacques Anquetil (2)	André Darrigade (2)	Imerio Massignan (2)	
49	1962	Jacques Anquetil (3)	Rudi Altig	Federico Bahamontes (4)	
50	1963	Jacques Anquetil (4)	Rik van Looy	Federico Bahamontes (5)	
51	1964	Jacques Anquetil (5)	Jan Janssen	Federico Bahamontes (6)	
52	1965	Felice Gimondi	Jan Janssen (2)	Julio Jiménez	
53	1966	Lucien Aimar	Willy Planckaert	Julio Jiménez (2)	
54	1967	Roger Pingeon	Jan Janssen (3)	Julio Jiménez (3)	
55	1968	Jan Janssen	Franco Bitossi	Aurelio González Puente	
56	1969	Eddy Merckx	Eddy Merckx	Eddy Merckx	
57	1970	Eddy Merckx (2)	Walter Godefroot	Eddy Merckx (2)	
58	1971	Eddy Merckx (3)	Eddy Merckx (2)	Lucien Van Impe	
59	1972	Eddy Merckx (4)	Eddy Merckx (3)	Lucien Van Impe (2)	
60	1973	Luis Ocaña	Herman van Springel	Pedro Torres	
61	1974	Eddy Merckx (5)	Patrick Sercu	Domingo Perurena	
62	1975	Bernard Thévenet	Rik Van Linden	Lucien Van Impe (3)	Francesco Moser
63	1976	Lucien Van Impe	Freddy Maertens	Giancarlo Bellini	Enrique Martínez Heredia
64	1977	Bernard Thévenet (2)	Jacques Esclassan	Lucien Van Impe (4)	Dietrich Thurau
65	1978	Bernard Hinault	Freddy Maertens (2)	Mariano Martínez	Henk Lubberding
66	1979	Bernard Hinault (2)	Bernard Hinault (2)	Giovanni Battaglin	Jean-René Bernaudeau
67	1980	Joop Zoetemelk	Rudy Pevenage	Raymond Martin	Johan van der Velde
68	1981	Bernard Hinault (3)	Freddy Maertens (3)	Lucien Van Impe (5)	Peter Winnen
69	1982	Bernard Hinault (4)	Sean Kelly	Bernard Vallet	Phil Anderson
70	1983	Laurent Fignon	Sean Kelly (2)	Lucien Van Impe (6)	Laurent Fignon
71	1984	Laurent Fignon (2)	Frank Hoste	Robert Millar	Greg LeMond
72	1985	Bernard Hinault (5)	Sean Kelly (3)	Luis Herrera	Fabio Parra
73	1986	Greg LeMond	Eric Vanderaerden	Bernard Hinault	Andrew Hampsten
74	1987	Stephen Roche	Jean-Paul van Poppel	Luis Herrera (2)	Raúl Alcalá
75	1988	Pedro Delgado	Eddy Planckaert	Steven Rooks	Erik Breukink
76	1989	Greg LeMond (2)	Sean Kelly (4)	Gert-Jan Theunisse	Fabrice Philipot
77	1990	Greg LeMond (3)	Olaf Ludwig	Thierry Claveyrolat	Gilles Delion
78	1991	Miguel Indurain	Djamolidine Abdoujaparov	Claudio Chiappucci	Álvaro Mejía Castrillón
79	1992	Miguel Indurain (2)	Laurent Jalabert	Claudio Chiappucci (2)	Eddy Bouwmans
80	1993	Miguel Indurain (3)	Djamolidine Abdoujaparov (2)	Tony Rominger	Antonio Martín
81	1994	Miguel Indurain (4)	Djamolidine Abdoujaparov (3)	Richard Virenque	Marco Pantani
82	1995	Miguel Indurain (5)	Laurent Jalabert (2)	Richard Virenque (2)	Marco Pantani (2)
83	1996	Bjarne Riis	Erik Zabel	Richard Virenque (3)	Jan Ullrich
84	1997	Jan Ullrich	Erik Zabel (2)	Richard Virenque (4)	Jan Ullrich (2)
85	1998	Marco Pantani	Erik Zabel (3)	Christophe Rinero	Jan Ullrich (3)
86	1999	Vacated[D]	Erik Zabel (4)	Richard Virenque (5)	Benoît Salmon
87	2000	Vacated[D]	Erik Zabel (5)	Santiago Botero	Francisco Mancebo
88	2001	Vacated[D]	Erik Zabel (6)	Laurent Jalabert	Óscar Sevilla
89	2002	Vacated[D]	Robbie McEwen	Laurent Jalabert (2)	Ivan Basso
90	2003	Vacated[D]	Baden Cooke	Richard Virenque (6)	Denis Menchov
91	2004	Vacated[D]	Robbie McEwen (2)	Richard Virenque (7)	Vladimir Karpets
92	2005	Vacated[D]	Thor Hushovd	Michael Rasmussen	Yaroslav Popovych
93	2006	Óscar Pereiro	Robbie McEwen (3)	Michael Rasmussen (2)	Damiano Cunego
94	2007	Alberto Contador	Tom Boonen	Mauricio Soler	Alberto Contador
95	2008	Carlos Sastre	Óscar Freire	Vacated	Andy Schleck
96	2009	Alberto Contador (2)	Thor Hushovd (2)	Franco Pellizotti	Andy Schleck (2)
97	2010	Andy Schleck	Alessandro Petacchi	Anthony Charteau	Andy Schleck (3)
98	2011	Cadel Evans	Mark Cavendish	Samuel Sánchez	Pierre Rolland
99	2012	Bradley Wiggins	Peter Sagan	Thomas Voeckler	Tejay van Garderen

Index

Acknowledgments

My thanks to: Lisa Thomas and Charlotte Atyeo at Bloomsbury, to Caroline Theakstone at Getty, to my agent David Luxton, to Daniel Friebe and, as always, to Virginie Pierret Moore, Brian and Jennifer Moore, Robin, Iciar and Kena, and Peter.

Picture credits

Jacket front: t Roger Viollet/Getty Images, 74266158; b Pascal Pavani/AFP/Getty Images, 121281254. Jacket back: tl Roger Viollet/Getty Images, 56227169; tr Phil Cole/Getty Images, 1250539; cl AFP/Getty Images, 51655774; cr Gamma-Rapho via Getty Images, 124130847; bl Doug Pensinger/Getty Images, 149041021; cr Brynn Lennon/Getty Images, 148993854.
2: Offside/L'Equipe, 253676; 4: Offside/L'Equipe, 220439; 7: Offside/L'Equipe, 27401; 8: AFP/Getty Images, 52009637; 10, Offside, 85955; 11: Doug Pensinger/Getty Images, 147867639; 12: Offside/L'Equipe, 193925; 14: Roger Viollet/Getty Images, 74267092; 16t: Roger Viollet/Getty Images, 56226701; 16b: Roger Viollet/Getty Images, 56227191; 17: Roger Viollet/Getty Images, 56227332; 18: Roger Viollet/Getty Images, 74267090; 19: Roger Viollet/Getty Images, 143373073; 20, Roger Viollet/Getty Images, 53129; 21: Roger Viollet/Getty Images, 74267301; 22: Offside/L'Equipe, 85973; 23: Offside/L'Equipe, 85974; 24t: Offside/L'Equipe, 194482; 24b: Offside/L'Equipe, 193923; 25: Offside/L'Equipe, 98035; 26t: Offside/L'Equipe, 98018; 26b: Offside/L'Equipe, 86374; 27: Offside/L'Equipe, 85989; 29: Offside/L'Equipe, 78064; 30, Offside/L'Equipe, 94349; 32: Roger Viollet/Getty Images, 74267277; 33t: AFP/Getty Images, 2054606; 33b: Roger Viollet/Getty Images, 74267281; 34: Getty Images, 3398583; 35: Getty Images, 3399133; 36: Gamma-Keystone via Getty Images, 107424369; 37: Roger Viollet/Getty Images, 74265636; 38t: Gamma-Keystone via Getty Images, 107424269; 38b: Offside/L'Equipe, 86074; 39: Offside/L'Equipe, 86064; 40t: Offside/L'Equipe, 86056; 40b: Offside/L'Equipe, 220431; 41: L'Equipe, 25842; 42: L'Equipe, 26060; 43: L'Equipe, 25846; 44: Offside/L'Equipe, 215496; 45: Offside/L'Equipe, 78062; 46: Offside/L'Equipe, 98041; 48: Roger Viollet/Getty Images, 74185746; 50t: Imagno/Getty Images, 99734441; 50b: Roger Viollet/Getty Images, 74227349; 51: Roger Viollet/Getty Images, 74225015; 52: Getty Images, 2927645; 53t: Gamma-Keystone via Getty Images, 107413477; 53b: Gamma-Keystone via Getty Images, 104402848; 54t: AFP/Getty Images, 96782619; 54b: Roger Viollet/Getty Images, 56205593; 55: Gamma-Keystone via Getty Images, 104419369; 56: Roger Viollet/Getty Images, 56205708; 57: Roger Viollet/Getty Images, 56226955; 58: Roger Viollet/Getty Images, 74225172; 59: Gamma-Keystone via Getty Images, 107413700; 60, L'Equipe, 39831; 61: Roger Viollet/Getty Images, 74225163; 62: L'Equipe, 20102; 63: Offside/L'Equipe, 98048; 64t: Gamma-Keystone via Getty Images, 106501305; 64b: Gamma-Keystone via Getty Images; 65: Roger Viollet/Getty Images, 74227185; 66: Getty Images, 155587084; 69: L'Equipe, 4696; 70: AFP/Getty Images, 91589679; 71t: Gamma-Keystone via Getty Images, 104402750; 71b: AFP/Getty Images, 93007623; 72: Pictorial Parade/Getty Images, 2927656; 73t: Roger Viollet/Getty Images, 74227345; 73b: Gamma-Keystone via Getty Images, 106500991; 74: AFP/Getty Images, 2031287; 75: Bert Hardy/Getty Images, 3435478; 76: Bert Hardy/Getty Images, 3301476; 77: Getty Images, 3242928; 78: Getty Images, 3379507; 79: Getty Images, 3380195; 80, Getty Images, 1. 155587083; 2. 118598326; 3.155587085; 4.155587085; 81: Gamma-Keystone via Getty Images, 104402845; 82: L'Equipe, 23606; 84: L'Equipe, 25818; 86t: Gamma-Keystone via Getty Images, 104402758; 86b: Roger Viollet/Getty Images, 74173487; 87: Gamma-Keystone via Getty Images, 104409187; 88: Popperfoto/Getty Images, 78962775; 89: Gamma-Keystone via Getty Images, 104402833; 90t: Roger Viollet/Getty Images, 74185735; 90b: Offside / L'Equipe, 4643; 91: AFP/Getty Images, 103135322; 92: Getty Images, 2927664; 93t: Roger Viollet/Getty Images, 74167285; 93b: Getty Images, 107411898; 94: AFP/Getty Images, 51959562; 95: AFP/Getty Images, 2031571; 96t: Popperfoto/Getty Images, 155364290; 96b: Gamma-Keystone via Getty Images, 104408239; 97: Offside/L'Equipe, 97563; 98: Offside/L'Equipe, 217642; 99t: Offside/L'Equipe, 23987; 99b: Offside/L'Equipe, 23723; 101tl: L'Equipe, 23550; 101tr: L'Equipe, 23551; 101bl: L'Equipe, 23552; 101br: L'Equipe, 23554; 104t, Gamma-Keystone via Getty Images, 105220440; 104b: Gamma-Keystone via Getty Images, 106505573; 105: Roger Viollet/Getty Images, 74167271; 106: Roger Viollet/Getty Images, 56227202; 107t, Central Press/Stringer/Getty Images, 3416350; 107b: Gamma-Keystone via Getty Images, 104402843; 108: Roger Viollet/Getty Images, 56227186; 109: Roger Viollet/Getty Images, 56227181; 110, Roger Viollet/Getty Images, 74166048; 111: Roger Viollet/Getty Images, 74173475; 112: Agence France Presse/Getty Images, 3142494; 113: Central Press/Getty Images, 118380781; 114: Popperfoto/Getty Images, 80752103; 115: Roger Viollet/Getty Images, 56227184; 116t: Popperfoto/Getty Images, 155364313; 116b: Popperfoto/Getty Images, 155364307; 117: RDA/

Getty Images, 155364315; 118: Popperfoto/Getty Images, 155364310; 119t: Popperfoto/Getty Images, 155364308; 119b: Keystone/Stringer/Getty Images, 155364309; 120, Offside/L'Equipe, 7558; 122l: Offside/L'Equipe, 7603; 122r: Offside/L'Equipe, 7604; 124t: AFP/Getty Images, 51655775; 124b: Popperfoto/Getty Images, 79664598; 125: AFP/Getty Images, 102098182; 126: AFP/Getty Images, 2030871; 127t: Keystone/Stringer/Getty Images, 3290678; 127b: AFP/Getty Images, 102097934; 128: AFP/Getty Images, 51959566; 129l: AFP/Getty Images, 51959556; 129r: AFP/Getty Images, 2116518; 130, AFP/Getty Images, 2746734; 131: McCabe/Stringer/Getty Images, 3135946; 132: Offside/L'Equipe, 98032; 133t: AFP/Getty Images, 2060555; 133b: Offside/L'Equipe, 69033; 134: AFP/Getty Images, 96712832; 135t: Offside/L'Equipe, 194484; 135bl: Offside/L'Equipe, 236973; 135br: Offside/L'Equipe, 236970; 136t: Popperfoto/Getty Images, 155364287; 136b: Popperfoto/Getty Images, 155364321; 137: Keystone/Stringer/Getty Images, 155364312; 138: Offside/L'Equipe, 50141; 140, Offside/L'Equipe, 108213; 142: AFP/Getty Images, 51656656; 143t: L'Equipe, 25911; 143b: Offside/L'Equipe, 231722; 144t: Gamma-Rapho via Getty Images, 124130847; 144b: Gamma-Rapho via Getty Images, 124130848; 145: Offside/L'Equipe, 47997; 146t: Offside/L'Equipe, 231041; 146b; , Offside/L'Equipe, 7641; 147: Offside/L'Equipe, 123403; 148t: Gamma-Keystone via Getty Images, 105220441; 148b: AFP/Getty Images, 103739467; 149: Offside / Pressesports, 223590; 150, Offside/L'Equipe, 44075; 151: Offside/L'Equipe, 97413; 152: AFP/Getty Images, 72570015; 154: AFP/Getty Images, 72570440; 156: AFP/Getty Images, 87255645; 157: Gamma-Rapho via Getty Images, 113989679; 158t: Offside/L'Equipe, 240565; 158b: Offside/L'Equipe, 240560; 159: Offside / Pressesports, 222478; 160, L'Equipe, 25762; 161: Offside/L'Equipe, 28392; 162: Offside/L'Equipe, 98029; 163: Bob Thomas/Getty Images, 155394845; 164: Bob Thomas/Getty Images, 155394843; 165: Bob Thomas/Getty Images, 155394846; 166: Bob Thomas/Getty Images, 155394844; 167: Offside/L'Equipe, 48618; 168: Offside/L'Equipe, 35135; 168b: Offside/L'Equipe, 252631; 169: Offside/L'Equipe, 196639; 170, Offside/L'Equipe, 98031; 172: Pascal Rondeau/Getty Images, 1762739; 174t: Pascal Rondeau/Getty Images, 1917659; 174b: Mike Powell/Getty Images, 1238502; 175: Alex Livesay/Getty Images, 1294247; 176t: Mike Powell/Getty Images, 1624583; 176b: Offside/L'Equipe, 27046; 177: Graham Chadwick/Getty Images, 156518171; 178: Graham Chadwick/Getty Images, 1637246; 179t, Alex Livesay/Getty Images, 1295184; 179b: Graham Chadwick/Getty Images, 1637274; 180, Mike Powell/Getty Images, 1915356; 181: Pascal Rondeau/Getty Images, 1622307; 182: Mike Powell/Getty Images, 1485734; 186: Tom Able-Green/Getty Images, 1046426; 187t: Doug Pensinger/Getty Images, 1485573; 187bl: Mike Powell/Getty Images, 725956; 187br: Olivier Morin/Getty Images, 51530122; 188: Doug Pensinger/Getty Images, 1020702; 189: Mike Powell/Getty Images, 1176018; 190, Offside, 107094; 191t: Offside/L'Equipe, 44535; 191b: Offside/L'Equipe, 44543; 192: Doug Pensinger/Getty Images, 2374883; 193: AFP/Getty Images, 2186016; 194: Robert Laberge/Getty Images, 2389292; 195: Patrick Kovarik//Getty Images, 51105905; 196t: Robert Laberge/Getty Images, 53193457; 196c: Robert Laberge/Getty Images, 53193460; 196b: Robert Laberge/Getty Images, 53193463; 197: Robert Laberge/Getty Images, 53217460; 198t: Offside, 44341; 198b: Doug Pensinger/Getty Images, 1020706; 199: Doug Pensinger/Getty Images, 1049338; 200, Doug Pensinger/Getty Images, 155394842; 201: Doug Pensinger/Getty Images, 1218037; 202: Offside/L'Equipe, 78009; 203tl: Offside/L'Equipe, 44788; 203tr: Offside/L'Equipe, 44789; 203bl: Offside/L'Equipe, 44801; 203br: Offside/L'Equipe, 44799; 204: Bryn Lennon/Getty Images, 71483103; 207: Bryn Lennon/Getty Images, 75271344; 208t: AFP/Getty Images, 75630598; 208b: Bryn Lennon/Getty Images, 75657024; 209: Bryn Lennon/Getty Images, 75446689; 210, Bryn Lennon/Getty Images, 75851454; 211t: AFP/Getty Images, 81903701; 211b: AFP/Getty Images, 8195336; 212t: AFP/Getty Images, 89019238; 212b: AFP/Getty Images, 89252271; 213: AFP/Getty Images, 102973474; 214t: Bryn Lennon/Getty Images, 102618529; 214b: Bryn Lennon/Getty Images, 119510794; 215: AFP/Getty Images, 118307043; 216: AFP/Getty Images, 119589908; 217t: Michael Steele/Getty Images, 118307358; 217c: Michael Steele/Getty Images, 119510639; 217b: John Berry/Getty Images, 149125943; 218t: Bryn Lennon/Getty Images, 148074538; 218b: Bryn Lennon/Getty Images, 148772816; 219: Bryn Lennon/Getty Images, 147995287.